Lessons in
Transforming Your Life

Book One

Marcia Grace

Disclaimer

The information in this book is provided for informational purposes only and is not a substitute for professional medical advice. The author and publisher make no legal claims, express or implied, and the material is not intended to replace the services of a physician.

The author, publisher and / or copyright holder assume no responsibility for the loss or damage caused, or allegedly caused, directly or indirectly by the use of information contained in this book. The author and publisher specifically disclaim any liability incurred from the use or application of the contents of this book.

Any resemblance of any names or characters, businesses or places, events or incidents to actual persons, living or dead or actual events, is purely coincidental and is simply from the perspective and opinion of the author.

Printed in the United States of America

First printing: March 2018

ISBN 978-0-9998400-1-6 (print)
ISBN 978-0-9998400-0-9 (ebook)
Higher Mind Press | Sound Beach, New York

Cover painting by Florida artist Linda Solomon. Her work delights my spirit.

Dedication

This book, and its companion volumes, were originally a series of blog posts. They are the result of a labor of love for my dear student and friend, Margaret Petro, who wanted these reflections to hold in her hand. I dedicate this book to her.

The blog itself and whatever wisdom it may contain, i attribute to my teacher, Dr. Kenneth Wapnick (1942–2013) who devoted his life to the study and teaching of the principles of *A Course in Miracles.* I am forever grateful to him and to his wife Gloria, who took over the daily operations of the business of disseminating Ken's teachings in books, audio, and video recordings with the expert assistance of Dr. Rosemarie LoSasso and Dr. Jeffrey Seibert.

Gratitude seems like such a puny word to describe my feelings for Helen Schucman and Bill Thetford who decided together to find "a better way" to be in the world. Their steadfast dedication to listening to and transcribing the words of the Voice that spoke to Helen in what she called "internal dictation" have given me the glorious opportunity to experience the peace of God in every moment of my day.

And to Judith Skutch Whitson, Robert Skutch, and Dr. William W. Whitson, founders of the Foundation for Inner Peace, and Tamara Morgan and Dr. Robert Rosenthal who will continue the work of the Foundation, i can only say, without your love for, trust in, and certainty of the power of the teachings of *A Course in Miracles*, nobody would ever have had the great gift of this transformative material.

I also want to gratefully acknowledge Marianne Williamson who, at an early age, gleaned the power of the Course and had the spiritual wherewithal to write *A Return to Love*, thereby presenting the metaphysical treatise of this age to the Sonship.

As no book meets the light of day without many helping hands, mine has had the dedicated touch of a number of people whose expertise and gentle guidance conspired to create this work in its present form: my editor/advisor Martha Bullen at Quantum Leap; my developmental editor, Heidi Grauel; and my book designer, Deana Riddle. Their compassion for a new author knows no bounds!

Also deserving of recognition for their willingness to be my first readers and disseminators of ideas, advice, corrections of grammar and location (or not) of commas, among other things: Jeanmarie Wilson (unofficial editor), Donna Trusnovec, Carrie Pollack, Keith Simmons, Linda Fostek, Linda Springer, Chris Tropin, Monica Bennett, Judy Cohen, Jay Morena, Meredith Gaffney, Rachel Love, Kathryn Hathaway, Trish Carr and Sorah Dubitsky. You are lights in my heaven!

Table of Contents

A portion of the revenue derived from this book will be donated to Heifer International, one of the top 10 charitable organizations. Founded in 1944, Heifer Project International works to end hunger and poverty and protect the earth. Through livestock, training and Passing on the Gift, Heifer has helped 30 million families in more than 125 countries improve their quality of life and move toward greater self-reliance. Heifer helps build strong communities because each project participant Passes on the Gift of their animal's first female offspring, training in its care and in sustainable agriculture to another family in need, multiplying the benefit.

If you would like a taste of the most important concepts that Marcia Grace teaches, go to http://www.MarciaGrace.com/3ways for a free download of:

"The 3 Ways We Keep Our Guilt, And How to Let It Go!"

Online Weekly Study Group with Marcia Grace

For Course students, or anyone wishing to begin an in-depth study of A Course in Miracles, I have set aside time to hold a weekly online class on the Zoom platform.

After you've gotten a good taste of the help you receive in understanding the Workbook lessons from CCJ, I sense that you may find a group study of the Text and Teacher's Manual equally useful in moving you toward your goal of calm, creativity and joyfulness.

The beauty of an online class is that you don't have to get dressed, then get in the car and drive somewhere in all kinds of weather. You have the benefit of being comfortable in your own chair with your favorite beverage while interacting (unless you don't want to—and there's a switch for that!) with other students in real time. The class will be limited so that everyone will have the opportunity to speak if they desire. We will read from the material and then I will translate ☺ what was just read! Class will begin in Spring, 2018

You can come for a month for a special discounted rate of $59. (I recommend this as the minimum to get yourself familiar with the language and concepts).

You can find out about other plans that are available, too, at http://MarciaGrace.com/course-miracles-online-class/ . There's absolutely no reason not to join our weekly discussions because you have a money-back guarantee!

If you want further clarity on the study group, (or anything else!), please email me at welcome@MarciaGrace.com . I look forward to meeting you online!

Peace Always,

Marcia Grace

Dear Sibling in Spirit,

Since you have chosen to open this book, it is my belief that being calm, creative, and joyful are important goals for you. Life is so much more rewarding when you can experience it without anxiety. Your creative juices flow easily and your relationships transform as your mind opens to new, more expansive possibilities. Daily contentment becomes your norm rather than an occasional surprise.

I honor your desire because i know that we all are part of something greater than our individual bodies and brains: something many call God, or Creation, or Universal Oneness, or Life. The word we use to describe this understanding of ourself as part of a larger whole is unimportant. Your experience of that oneness is all-important. And it is through nurturing that experience that you will come to be the calm, creative, and joyful person you are destined to be!

This, and the companion books in this series, come from my many years of study and contemplation of A Course in Miracles. My intention is to share the gifts this spiritual work of art and high philosophy have given me. I can affirm what the yoga teacher who told me about ACIM in 1978 said, "It has changed my life!"
In these pages, we're going to work on some serious stuff! We'll uncover:

- a *radical* teaching that asks us to suspend every belief we have in order to allow space for new ideas to grow.

- the great metaphysical treatise of the current era.

- an answer to humanity's ancient question, "How did we get here?"

- the philosophical, psychological, and spiritual dilemma of what we call *life*: who we are and who we think we are.

- the misperceptions in our minds that cause us continual discomfort, often agony and always fear (if we're really honest with ourselves).

The Workbook of *ACIM* contains 365 lessons—theoretically, one lesson to be done each day for a year, although the time it takes you to complete the lessons is secondary to the commitment you make to learning them. Although it is certainly not necessary, i encourage you to read the lesson from the Workbook, too. If you are unable to read one lesson every day, notice the guilt feelings that may arise. Affirm they are simply thoughts in your separated mind, and are not real!

You will find one or more exercises at the end of each lesson, so I highly recommend you use a notebook to write in as you go along.

At the beginning of the book you will find a glossary of what I think are the most misunderstood terms in the Course. The redefining of words throughout the material can lead the unprepared reader into a state of confusion! If you read a passage that doesn't seem to make sense, check the glossary to see if the term has been redefined.

Each time i do a lesson, i discover a new layer of resistance to peace for me to look at. This *is* the journey of this book! We are learning to let go of fear, so we can truly love.

Doing this series was a pledge to my Self to set aside quiet time to read the lesson and write my thoughts. I offer you the opportunity to make the same pledge to your Self. Through our study and reflection of these life-changing lessons, we grow in God's Love together. And, by the time you finish reading this book, you will have many of the tools that will help you achieve the calm, creative, and joyful life you desire!

God is Love,
Marcia Grace

Author's Note: A word about my writing "tics." In the middle of a sentence, i use the lower case "i" when speaking of myself just as i would use you, her, him, his, she, etc. I have adopted the singular form "s/he" (for she/he) and "hir" (for him/her) to include everyone.

Also, because my goal is to encourage our recognition of *oneness*, i write mostly in the first-person plural to be all inclusive, such as, *ourself* rather than ourselves.

Oh, Holy One,

I walk toward you, trembling and stumbling,

Tired and worn with cares.

I do not know the way

But Your light glimmers faintly

in the distance.

Something, an indistinct whisper,

a gentle nudge

Is showing me the path.

I wander off repeatedly

But Your Voice grows in my awareness

And calls me back.

I am grateful

for Your your endless Love and Guidance.

Glossary

Note: There are many terms in the material that we think we comprehend because they stem from Christianity. However, here they are given new definitions. This is a basic list. If, as you read, you are unclear about the meaning of a word, it may be because this word is being used in a new way. I'd be grateful if you would email the word or term to me to be included in the next edition.

Atonement The process of correcting the mistaken beliefs we have. Because we are on ego-automatic, our beliefs initially are based in fear. Our study will teach us how to shift our perception to our right mind where old fears are replaced with calm and certainty.

Ego-automatic This is a term i coined to express our lack of desire to challenge our belief that we are victims of a cold, cruel world, helpless to stem the tide of destructive forces heading in our direction.

Ego/Wrong Mind ACIM states that our mind is split. Part of our mind (ego) seems to be contained in the area of the body we call the brain and is separate and distinct from all other minds. Yet, there is another part of our mind that remains connected to its Source.

Forgiveness This is the numero uno, head of the class, irreplaceable, unparalleled tool we are given to accomplish the goal of the *Course*: the peace of God. Because of its supreme importance to our success, I will explain what it is and how to use it over the course of these lessons. We need to tread slowly that we may fully understand the implications of true forgiveness. (It's not what you think!) Suffice it to say, in these early lessons, as we open our hearts and minds to this new way of thinking, we will begin to uncover the true nature of forgiveness!

God Defining the concept of "God" is much too rich and detailed to enter here. Just let me say that God is not a person with a body and a set of characteristics as the Bible describes. In our study, God is eternal, without limit, and indivisible: First Cause of the Effect of Creation (Us). As such, S/he/It did not create the ego, which is an illusion.

Holy Spirit/Right Mind The active principle of creation. H.S. resides in the right part of our mind which is always connected to God, the Source. The goal of this work is to teach us to shift our thoughts to the right mind so we can hear the guidance of the Holy Spirit. Hir guidance will bring us peace in the form we can accept at the moment.

Jesus Unlike traditional Christianity, which teaches that Jesus is the only Son of God, this *Course* makes it clear that Jesus is our *elder brother*. He is wiser because of his experience, but our equal as members of the Sonship of God's creation.

Judgment The ego's effort to maintain separation from other minds by regarding them as better or worse than itself. The ego evaluates the bodies of others based on fear, and, therefore, can never experience equality.

Miracle A change of perception, from thoughts of separation to thoughts of unity; from fear thoughts to thoughts of acceptance and love.

Teacher Spelled with an uppercase T, our Teacher is the "consciousness" (for lack of a better word) that resides in our right mind and is connected to our Source. S/he is the author of these lessons as well as our Guide, if we are willing to listen! (Can be equated with Jesus and the Holy Spirit.)

Time An essential concept in this *Course*. According to our Teacher, because God is eternal and indivisible, time must be an illusion. How can something eternal have a past or a future?

Veil of Forgetfulness A term representing the desire on the part of the ego to bury the mind's true nature under a façade of materiality.

Lesson 1

Nothing I see [in this room, on this street, from this window, in this place] means anything.

Did i mention that this *Course* is *radical*?! Even after 30+ years of practice, i am shocked by the implications of this first lesson. Right now, i'm looking at pictures of my family—my children, my grandchildren—and i'm supposed to say they don't mean anything?! Yet, i continue looking about the room and repeating the lesson indiscriminately. Even so, the ego is chattering in the background: "Liar! my DVD player means a lot to me. So, does the wood stove merrily burning away, keeping me warm, and the cat, curled up next to me is my precious!" Yet, i continue glancing around a moment longer, then close the book.

Of course, i know that there is a purpose behind this seemingly unbelievable statement, but it still grabs my ego's attention and rattles its cage, and always will.

With this lesson, we begin the process of removing value from the "valueless." If we *are* truly spirit as the *Course* assures us we are, then this body that i seem to inhabit cannot be my reality and is no more important than the chair or the pen. This does not mean that we should not take care of the body but it does mean that we must re-examine very clearly how we use it as we go about our day.

Reader Reflection/Action

What was the first thing that came to mind when you read this lesson? Just notice the thought and let it go. Consider how many people and things have come and gone in your life, and you are still here!

Author's Note: At this early stage, it is best to "fake it till you make it" and not become too heavily invested in trying to figure out what these early lessons mean. It is also a good idea to refrain from arguing against the lesson. If anything about this *Course* is drawing you to dip your toe in (and since you are here, i would say that is the case!), then proceed!! And be as gentle with yourself as possible.

Lesson 2

I have given everything I see in this room [on this street, from this window, in this place] all the meaning that it has for me.

Ahhh, this lesson is a relief after yesterday! This statement makes complete sense to me. I've been around long enough to notice two people can look at the same thing and have two different opinions. Even my own opinion of something changes with new information. Therefore, it is obvious that each of us perceives everything and everyone uniquely, in each moment. And no two moments are quite the same because our input is always in a dynamic state—altering continuously due to stimuli seemingly external as well as internal. The weather, the light, my stomach growling, sounds i hear, tasks needing attention, etc., etc. all swirling around in our mind like a kaleidoscope of images. Yes, the uncomfortable feelings of yesterday's lesson are appeased by this very sensible assertion.

However, a sneaking suspicion comes to mind—there is something more to this statement than my first assumption. In my first reading, intellectually i could grasp that i wouldn't know what a cup was without previous interaction with it. Yet, making the transition to living things from inanimate objects seemed unrelated. The instructions move from inanimate to animate objects as if they were the same. Consider the value of "a body or a button." I would think it normal to consider a body more important than a button, right? It would seem so, but i'll leave my mind open to all possibilities.

Reader Reflection/Action ~

Can you see how you assign different levels and degrees of importance to the people and things around you? Make a list of the 10 things you value the most, ranked by their importance.

Lesson 3

I do not understand anything I see in this room [on this street, from this window, in this place].

Another shocking statement, although less so than Lesson 1, or perhaps i am adjusting to the idea of radical statements from this *Course*! How can anything as obvious and easily observed as a dresser or a philodendron not be understandable? I remember thinking the first time around (in November 1978), "Have i left my senses doing this crazy book that makes ridiculous statements?" (The answer is of course, *yes*!) But something, a curiosity, a doubt about the validity of my thoughts, a profound feeling that there was Truth (with a capital T) in this incomprehensibility, kept me going.

"The point of the exercises is to help you clear your mind of all past associations." "OK," i say to myself, and notice the flood of thoughts that accompany each glance at an object around the room. What is now obvious to me is that i have so many past associations of *everything i look at*. This is a revelation! (Well, not quite, but definitely an eye-opener!)

Now i begin to see the plan behind this lesson. We are to withhold judgment, to keep an open mind, as we look around the room. So, there is a connection between the past and judgment . . . hmmm. This is eminently logical. I have placed a judgment upon occurrences in the past based on my mental state at the time. Then i carry that judgment into the present without alteration even though i may be in a very different mental state now. So, am i really in the present? And if i am not in the present, then clearly i cannot truly understand what i see now. This is interesting, indeed!

We are gently being introduced to a radically new concept of time. This concept is the glue that holds the whole thought system of this *Course* together.

Reader Reflection/Action ~

Is there anything from Lesson 1 that you've looked upon differently today? As you scan your surroundings, what are your thoughts? Write them down, if you wish. Imagine someone you dislike. Now, think of that person without any past association. What do you see?

Lesson 4

These thoughts do not mean anything. They are like the things I see in this room [on this street, from this window, in this place].

This is a major lesson aimed at helping us separate the meaningful from the meaningless. Spend a minute or so watching your thoughts and then apply the idea for today to each thought you recognize.

Quoting again from the *Introduction*, "Remember only this: you need not believe the ideas, you need not accept them, and you need not even welcome them. Some of them you might actively resist. None of this will matter or decrease their efficacy . . . whatever your reactions to the ideas may be, use them."

On my initial reading of this, i wanted to argue with the statement. It's one thing to admit that i have given my interpretation to the things i see and that my thoughts about specific things may be wrong occasionally, but to be told that all my thoughts both good and bad are as meaningless as the things i see is another shock to my ego.

This lesson makes it clear that we are to equate the *thoughts* in our mind with the *things* we see around us—and all are equally meaningless! Oy vey, as they say in France! Here we are again, confronting the very core of our belief system. ("This is not work for cowards," my first ACIM teacher Paul Steinberg often intoned.) It is not surprising that feelings of utter worthlessness were quickly rising to the surface producing an inner cringing sensation in my mind. At this early stage of learning, my ego was most often likely to win the battle for my consciousness!

Today's ideas were like a sledge hammer cracking open my ego defenses and laying bare a new born willingness to "see things differently." And this generated a second alarm—one that produced an astonishing thought—i had had no awareness of those feelings of worthlessness until i read this lesson! Therefore, what i was beginning to understand was that i am not aware of many (if not most) of my thoughts until some catalyst unearths them! So, despite my reservations concerning this lesson, i decided that the writer was smarter than me! I could feel truth in this statement. Therefore, i would put my bruised feelings aside for a while.

On later readings i felt a great sense of freedom, a weight lifting, in hearing that my thoughts don't mean anything. With this expanded consciousness i could truly begin to look at my thoughts critically to determine their value, and dialogue with the Holy Spirit as to their validity. This has now become a practice i engage in throughout the day.

Having spent so many years doing meditation, i can be "thoughtless" for long periods yet i often experience physiological interruptions (which are still thoughts: "i'm hungry," "i'm getting a cramp," etc.). These are what i used in this exercise today.

Reader Reflection/Action ~

Did your ego object as harshly as mine did to this lesson? Are you finding it easier to separate your thoughts so that you can see each one? This is one of the major benefits of doing these lessons. If you can access your thoughts, you can decide to release the ones that are hurting you. Are you willing to accept that your beliefs about the people and circumstances in your life may be incorrect?

Lesson 5

I am never upset for the reason I think.

Now i understand why i kept doing these lessons way back in 1978—I loved being shocked! This is a mindboggling statement for someone who thinks s/he knows what motivates hir. My child spilled the milk; my boss blamed me for something i didn't do; my best friend died; i may have cancer, etc., etc. These are all worthy items for upset, per my ego.

And this belief remains "until you learn that form does not matter." I glossed over the form issue for many years yet, over time, it became clear to me that i give different degrees of meaning to every form i see. This being the case, i am obviously not "recognizing they are all the same." (W5.1:6)

This *Course* seems to be asking the impossible of me: to believe that *everything in this world is the same*. All things that i see and thoughts that i think are simply variations on the theme of separation. And, if everything is the same (in that they are not real), then my reason for being upset at certain distinct things has no merit. Philosophically and intellectually, i can agree; to intuit this on an emotional level often takes a lifetime. Yet, i can see the advantage of believing this and putting it into practice in my life.

I think it was on my second time around that i realized our Teacher was brainwashing us with these lessons. But brainwashing to eliminate the brain (which is part of the body/brain continuum of the ego) and its false thoughts in order to reveal the spirit hidden under the "veil of forgetfulness." As long as we categorize and compare the specific events in our day, we hold on to the pain that invariably results.

Reader Reflection/Action ~

What is the last thing you were upset about? After this lesson, does it still feel valid? As you go through your day, attempt to observe your emotions as they arise. You may find that the simple act of "noticing" will bring about a shift in your perspective so that the feeling subsides, leaving you calm. This is a miracle!

Author's Note: Here we receive simple instruction—do this, don't do that, and so on. We are to take these ideas whether we understand them, or agree with them, or not, and apply them to our moment to moment experiences. I certainly got the distinct feeling that i was not to question the lesson too forcefully as it would not be in my own best interest. I felt this intuitively more than knew it as fact.

Lesson 6

I'm upset because I see something that is not there.

Today's lesson seems very much like Lesson 2 in that i have given what i see "all the meaning that it has for me." As a result, how real can my perception be since i could easily find a number of people who would have a different perception of the very same thing i seem to be seeing?

We are like little children who come rushing into the room yelling, "Mommy, Mommy! Junior just broke my toy!" and Mom says, "Oh, that's such a shame! You must be very upset. Here, let's see if we can fix it." Both of us are looking at the same broken toy but from a very different point of view.

"The upset may seem to be fear, worry, depression, anxiety, anger, hatred, jealousy or any number of forms . . . which will be perceived as different. This is not true." It didn't take me too long (maybe 5 years) to catch myself in one of these states and ask for correction. What took much longer was realizing that pride and joy (the momentary kind) are also not there because they are all temporary states.

As we learn later, anything that is temporal is not real because it is not eternal. And, if it is not real (since it is a capricious state that will soon pass), then it cannot be *present*. Therefore, it is "not there." An example: I'm in the supermarket standing in line. Someone pushes in front of me just as i'm about to put my items on the counter. "I have to get to the bus to pick up my kid," says the person. My old self (the ego) would feel put upon (furious!) and have a snappy reply. My right-minded self, however, would take the anger that arises and immediately seek its correction. And then it would be gone. So, was the anger real?

With these lessons, we are embarking on a Self-directed course. The Holy Spirit, and his alter ego our brother Jesus (our Teacher), are our internal GPS that can only operate if we turn it on.

Reader Reflection/Action ~

What temporary state have you been giving too much importance? Think about someone with whom you disagree. Attempt to put yourself in hir shoes. What do you notice?

Lesson 7

I see only the past.

Today it seems as though i'm doing a jigsaw puzzle and each day i manage to fit another piece into its place. The individual piece has its own shape and size but when it's put in its proper space, its edges seem to disappear as the colors flow from one to the other.

Here comes another shocker! This seventh lesson is the basis of the first six. I don't understand anything, i'm never upset for the reason i think, my thoughts are meaningless, etc. because everything i think and do is based on my past experience and my thoughts about them. "Everything you believe is rooted in time." (W7.2) What else is there? my ego wants to know.

Our brother Jesus is a gentle teacher, yet he insists on a few things.

1. That we do only one lesson a day. For most of us this is a difficult enough.

And for the type A personalities who are driven to do more than one lesson a day, it is important to remember that speed does not equal success, but it does succeed in splitting the focus, which is the ego's goal.

And for the perfectionists who won't go on to the next lesson until they get it right—just go on! The ego will do everything in its power to prevent our completing these lessons. Acknowledge the distraction and go on!

2. That we be as indiscriminate as possible in applying the lesson to objects around us. We will probably experience many mixed feelings. It is good to notice how we want to linger on some objects and ignore others. "Old ideas are difficult to change."

3. That we must not judge or interpret the lesson but simply do what it says. This is a course in mind training. "An untrained mind can accomplish nothing." (W Intro 1:3) In doing these lessons we begin to see how undisciplined our thoughts are—what the Buddhists call "monkey mind." If we truly understood the lessons, we would not need to do them.

Reader Reflection/Action ~

Choose something you are upset about, then spend some time sitting with your feelings about this person or situation. Is there another way you could see hir? How might your life be different if you weren't upset about that person or situation?

Lesson 8

My mind is preoccupied with past thoughts.

Today's lesson builds on yesterday's statement that we see only the past. What the body's eyes see is determined by the thoughts in our mind. Our thoughts manifest the entire world and all its inhabitants that we experience. Work to connect thoughts with things: the kind of thoughts we allow in our mind will produce a commensurate world—peaceful thoughts bring a considerate world whereas angry, frightened thoughts dictate a destructive chaotic world. These early lessons help us start to question the validity as well as the quality of our thinking.

A good reason why today's idea is almost incomprehensible is because of our self-hatred: we hate the self we think we are. We feel bad about ourself and cover it over with grandiose concepts of who and what we are. Our ego never admits this antipathy, but it is evident in the way we live our life. We see difficulties everywhere and enemies at the ready to crush us. We feel overwhelmed by forces "outside" of us. Our ego teaches that we are victims of a cruel and indifferent world.

The purpose of these early lessons is to disrupt the complacency of the ego with statements like: "Very few have realized what is entailed in picturing the past or anticipating the future. The mind is actually blank when it does this, because it is not really thinking about anything." (W8.2:3-4) I would have sworn mightily that that sentence was not there the first time i read the lesson. My frigid thinking could not "see" what it couldn't comprehend.

The ego is *not* who we are. "No one really sees anything" means our ego thought system is incapable of experiencing reality. The ego writes a script and then proceeds to play it out. The people and things we see around us are the figments of our miscreative efforts. It is important to note that emotions are as unreal as any other thoughts since they also stem from past memories.

Observe your thoughts. It is that function of self-awareness that allows us to notice the error of our thinking *without guilt* so that we may "choose once again" and in that new choice experience the peace of God. This certainly cannot happen until we realize that we can get off the glacier that is the ego thought system and return to the enveloping warmth and limitless peace of our Creator.

Reader Reflection/Action ~

How is the teaching in this lesson different from meditation? Write down three things that upset you that you've accepted as true for a long time. How do you know they are still "true"? Make an effort, as you go about your day, saying to yourself each time you observe a thought, "I *seem* to be thinking about . . .."

Author's Note: There is another facet to our True Self that is being uncovered and nurtured with these lessons. At this stage, it is but an inkling, a minute flash of light reflected from the icicles hanging from our image-laden mind. A part of our mind is beginning to chip away at the frozen layers of fantasy the ego has thus far successfully perpetrated to keep us in its tightly coiled grasp. Yet an unfamiliar warmth is insinuating itself into our awareness.

Lesson 9

I see nothing as it is now.

Am i willing to accept that i do not understand what i see? My ego is thumping its chest and shouting at me to stop all this nonsense about what i'm seeing not being real. "Look, you can touch the table, knock on it, it's wood, you know that! Pinch your leg, it hurts, right?!" Yet, the lesson states, "You do not need to practice what you already understand. It would indeed be circular to aim at understanding, and assume you have it already." (W9.1:7)

Something deep inside reassures me, "You were led to this *Course* because you were ready to go beyond the five-sensory world that seems so concrete yet is filled with endless contradictions and needless pain. There is something more. A loving Creator would never put you through such suffering." Therefore, against my ego's wishes, i admit i see nothing as it is now. There is a calm that comes with this decision even though i have no idea where it will take me.

If there is one thing the ego hates, it's being wrong. You know that churning in the gut that you get when you realize you've made a mistake? This is the major stumbling block to achieving the peace of God for which this *system* was designed.

The *Course* is not about transcendence but rather *transformation*. It does not aim for Heaven but for peace on earth. We are here to make the choice to change our mind about the world we see, "to lighten every corner of the mind that has been cleared of the debris that darkens it." (W9.2:5)

Our Teacher makes it very clear that we must first heal our mind of the belief in separation in order to *resume our rightful place with God*. We've manufactured an alternative universe of bodies and buildings, of sun and snow, of friendship and war. We see nothing as it is *now* because we have chosen the hell of duality and time instead. This choice requires correction.

We've never left Heaven, so we don't need to get there. "Heaven is here. There is nowhere else. Heaven is now. There is no other time." (M24.6:4-7) *Now* is when we know this. And we cannot know anything true until we release our thoughts of the past, recognizing them for what they really are: blocks to the awareness of love's presence (in the present!)

"What I have chosen to see has cost me vision. Now I would choose again that I may see." (W52.4:5-6)

Reader Reflection/Action ~

Is there something you're glad to remove past judgment and meaning from? To *release*? Maybe trust is difficult for you. Why do you think that's so? Whom do you trust? Can you envision how wonderful it would be to see that all the judgmental thoughts you think you're thinking have no effect and are nothing at all? You are exchanging the darkness of guilt for the light of vision!

Lesson 10

My thoughts do not mean anything.

This lesson looks familiar because it is almost a duplicate of Lesson 4. The repetition of a lesson indicates its great importance. I mentioned before that these early lessons are ice breakers meant to plunge us immediately into a new way of thinking. This can only be accomplished by discerning our current thoughts and finding them lacking. We cannot have two opposing thoughts in mind at the same time. Therefore, it is crucial to recognize the quality of a thought in order to keep it or let it go.

Our Teacher speaks to us from two opposing points of view because we are invested in duality and will not let it go until we see its harmfulness rather than its benefits. There is only truth and no illusion—this is the place in mind we are striving toward.

In our current stage of consciousness, however, there are many levels to what we call "reality" but all are images we have made. In a sense, we are experiencing ourself as schizophrenic—we see things that aren't there. The mind seems to be split between two unrelated states of reality. This is what Jesus means when he refers to us as "insane." "Anyone who elects a totally insane guide (the ego) must be totally insane himself." (T9. IV.8:4) Yet, we will have as many levels of "reality" as is necessary until we achieve mastery of our mind.

Think back to your early childhood; remember some of the concerns you had that seemed monumental at the time but now make not the slightest blip on your anxiety scale? Move forward in time to the teenage years. Recall the passion of new ideas that sent you flying off in all directions at once, there not being enough hours in the day to do it all. And the snooty kid in school who wouldn't talk to you was really just as shy as you were. Now you chuckle at the internal image of those frenetic years. They have no meaning to you today.

And so, on as we follow the trail through the forest of our life we realize the sound we thought was a bear behind us was simply a twig cracked underfoot by a companion. And that dark spot on the ground ahead was not a hole that led down to hell where we would fry. That high-pitched howl was not a wolf coming to take a chunk out of our throat but only a night owl. All these fearful thoughts seemed so terrifyingly real. But where are they now?

Our brother Jesus tells us that we are not yet able to truly compare a real thought and an illusion. He says, "When you do, you will have no doubt that what you once believed were your thoughts did not mean anything." However, we *can* use our memory of past events to demonstrate how our thoughts change over time, until there is no time that we do not feel the enfolding love of our Source.

Each time i can say "My thought about ___ does not mean anything," i am choosing to expand my consciousness, to become more inclusive rather than exclusive, to open a mental space for a new way of being in the world. In this new world, the forest is a lush and green paradise filled with peace and beauty rather than a danger-filled trap of darkness and fear.

Reader Reflection/Action ~

In quiet today, close your eyes and spend some time watching your thoughts. Discern if they are helpful or hurtful to you. Would you be upset if others could hear your thoughts?

Lesson 11

My meaningless thoughts are showing me a meaningless world.

Much as my ego would like to soften the impact of statements like this, the fact remains that this *Course* is radical! (I think i said that before!) It proclaims its motivation as, "The reversal of the thinking of the world." (W11.1) It states categorically that it is our *thoughts* that determine the world we see, not the world that determines our thoughts. In other words, the cause of my upset is not anything i see outside myself. The cause of my upset stems from a belief in my mind. WOW!!!! Merely trying to digest this excessively large thought is cause for upset (for my ego, that is). The tactic i took on the first pass through this exotic terrain was simply to shake my head and keep on reading.

I can remember a sense of capitulation upon reading these words the first time. The arguing and rationalizing began to take a backseat to a new and unsettling feeling of dismay. Part of me acknowledged that everything i had read thus far was true yet i had a sense of helpless hopelessness. How could little insignificant me have the power to change the way i saw the people and situations in my world?

The ego's understanding of power is complex (as are most things to the ego, which thrives on convolution). Reading this lesson, it derides us saying, "How arrogant of you to think you could be the all-powerful driver of your life! You know you have no control over others and hardly any over yourself." Depending upon our individual script, we have one of two possible responses to this: either we submit to our learned vulnerability and tiptoe through life trying to stay out of trouble, blaming everyone and everything around us for our difficulties; or we flaunt the self-talk and go crashing through each moment ready for a fight, asserting power and strength. In either case, we are sublimating the feelings of worthlessness that we have accepted because we've taken the ego's hand.

Yet there is great hope in the sentences: "Be glad to practice the idea . . . for in it is your release made sure. The key to forgiveness lies in it." This is a positive promise and forgiveness (see the glossary) plays a major role although we may not be sure exactly who or what is to be forgiven yet. It offers a tantalizing assertion of good things to come. And, indeed, there are, and continues to be, endless good things ahead.

The lessons are beautifully balanced. We are first given a mind-expanding (and often unsettling) idea followed by loving reassurance. As in this lesson we are told it is "the foundation for the peace, relaxation, and freedom from worry that we are trying to achieve." And here we get the purpose of our *Course*: the attainment of peace. That's all i needed to hear to keep me in the role of a willing student.

Reader Reflection/Action ~

Is there something you previously *knew* was meaningless, but this lesson helped you to fully recognize and own that knowledge? Also, what is your definition of forgiveness? Write it down and keep it for further reference.

Lesson 12

I am upset because I see a meaningless world.

"I'm upset."—the emotion; "I see a meaningless world."—the correction.

I'm not upset because i know i'm looking at a meaningless world. I'm upset because i believe in what i see and what i see is chaotic. The aim of this lesson is to realize i'm upset over innumerable images i have manufactured that are all equally nonexistent.

Here i am instructed to gaze about my surroundings giving equal time to every, bar none, object that my eyes rest upon because they are all equally unreal. Jesus iterates several times that i must include "good" as well as "bad" things in my perusal as they *all* are the same.

This lesson continues the ongoing theme that our thoughts make the world rather than the reverse. We assign it scary, sad, violent, or insane interpretations as well as happy, exciting, or satisfying ones. "The world is meaningless in itself." (W12.1:4) The introduction of the addition of "good" thoughts adds more seasoning to the soup of concepts being blended in the kettle of our mind. Ah, so it's not just my bad thoughts that aren't real . . . my good thoughts aren't either! I feel the rug moving!!!

We are being gently guided to do what Buddhists call "detaching from the world." (I've heard the *Course* defined as "Christian Zen.") Detaching in *Course* terms means recognizing our unreal thoughts about the world so we can have them corrected by the Holy Spirit. In the clear space left, we will see our real thoughts when we choose to think with God: thoughts of love, peace, and joy.

In the chicken or egg query, the chicken (the ego) in this case, definitely comes before the egg (the world). Later we will learn that this applies to God as well—God comes first (the chicken) and His Creation meaning us (the egg) comes next. God created us, we didn't create God. This becomes very important in truly understanding two foundational principles of this *Course*: 1. We cannot usurp God's power, and 2. We cannot be separate from God. Then chicken and egg merge into the oneness they always are.

Reader Reflection/Action ~

How do you perceive the meaninglessness of the world? List five things that are meaningless in your life right now. Think of a recurring theme in your life—can't lose weight, my job sucks, my spouse/parent/child doesn't understand me. Close your eyes and imagine that repetitive thought as a slimy leech attached to your leg. Yuck, right? You cannot go anywhere until you remove that parasite from your body. You cannot see beyond your leg because all you can think about is getting rid of this horrid distraction. You find a utensil and scrape the worm off your leg. Ahhhh, relief! Now you can move forward (after you squash it flat!). Do this exercise with as many of your meaningless thoughts as you can stomach!

Lesson 13

A meaningless world engenders fear.

Today's lesson introduces a central idea in the *Course's* ontology: we are here in this world because we believe we are "in competition with God." Competition assumes duality. One must have another to compete against.

The ego tells us that God is *other* and takes on a threatening nature. "A meaningless world engenders fear because I think I am in competition with God." (W13.4:7) He is angry when we do bad things, as is well documented in early Biblical stories. Since we so often find ourself doing bad things (as we perceive our separated self), we must then assume that God is angry with us. We then fear this dangerous god and keep choosing to stay as far away from him as possible *by staying in the world.* The world thus becomes a refuge from this avenging god who will annihilate us should we ever get close enough to him, says the ego.

The brief story i just outlined of our separation from God seems insane. Aren't most of us taught in our childhood religions that God is a loving God and only wants our happiness?

But i always asked myself if that were true, then why is there so much suffering in the world? Free will wasn't a satisfactory answer. The Bible attests to this. We are here because we disobeyed God and ate the fruit from the tree of knowledge. In His anger at our sin, He kicked us out of the Garden to live and die in pain and suffering.

The *Course's* creation story says just the opposite: we have always had and continue to have God's knowledge, being part of Him. Yet we had a "tiny mad idea" that there could be something outside of God's Love, which we took seriously. The Son of God (us) "remembered not to laugh" at this false premise. The world of bodies and time we seem to be inhabiting is the result of that insane idea. Out of our fear we split off our reality and invented an alternate state of being in which to hide from an imagined angry God.

In making this world, we gave up the knowledge of our True Identity as God's holy creation. We have subsumed What we are, *as eternal Being*, under a mantle of false images. We give them meaning by our belief in them. A while back i heard about an interesting study using radiologists who are highly paid for their great observational skills. They are able to find a tiny tumor in an X-ray that most of us could not detect. A total of 85% of the radiologists tested didn't notice the elephant that had been placed in the middle of the X-ray. The researchers attributed this to the fact that they weren't looking for an elephant and so they didn't see it. Reiterating Lesson 6: "... i see something that is not there" or vice versa. We see what we want to see.

So why would we want to make up an illusory world? In the Garden of Eden story, God kicks A & E (us) out because of their (our) transgression. The *Course*, on the other hand, says we *chose* to leave Heaven believing we had sinned against

God because we thought, "Could there be something beyond God?" The guilt borne of this idea sent us scurrying away to find a dark hiding place where a very angry Father could not come. In denying God's love and protection, we seemingly made ourself the master of an alternative universe, in competition with God. Fear makes our world go 'round because we know, in our heart of hearts, that God will one day catch up with us and then it will all be over. So saith the ego. None of this is true says our Teacher, yet we continue to believe it because we love our autonomy.

We are doing the lessons so that we remember to value the right mind over the ego. Eventually, we realize that God is not challenging us, but we, in our wrong—or ego—mind, are choosing to be distant from God. This is a wonderful realization because, if we chose separation because of a false belief based in fear, we can shift our thinking to align with the truth of our eternal union with our Source. That is the reality of peace.

Reader Reflection/Action

How has your ego kept you from God, from peace? Can you uncover some of the fearful thoughts in your mind that hide the truth about you? Who would you be without your righteous indignation against [fill in the blank]? Now, bring up a fond memory. A good feeling comes with it, right? What's to stop you from bringing that good feeling into the next moment and the next in your day?

Lesson 14

God did not create a meaningless world.

Here is the reason why the last 13 lessons have focused on our thoughts as meaningless. It is crucial that we recognize our unreal (ego) thoughts so that we can eliminate "the blocks to the awareness of love's presence." (Into to the Text)

Jesus implies that we are well aware that the world we have manifested as an escape from God is completely meaningless. But having accepted the ego as our guide, we have elected to favor the existence of dualism as our reality. In a dualistic world, God is good and we are bad. In that case, the meaninglessness of the ego's beliefs must be denied and rationalized. Therefore, our "badness" is projected outward, with perpetual chaos disguised as "the vicissitudes of life."

As i mentioned on Day 13, our mind is split so we are initially choosing the ego thought system, pushing our true nature under the nearest bush. It is safe to say that as long as we believe in the importance of things in the world, we are thinking with the ego. Jesus' statement, "The world you see has nothing to do with reality. It is of your own making, and it does not exist," (W14.1:4-5) couldn't be said more clearly. Do we have ears to hear?

It is probably easier to accept this at first in a personal manner. "Ok," i say to myself, "I can see that some of my thoughts are ridiculous," but to say, "God did not create that war, and so it is not real," seems impossible to accept. Let it go for now and note that these "universal" ideas are "shared illusions." Since we seem to be many, we find allies who share our beliefs in order to give them validity. Our fear of confronting the truth, which we know lies beneath the chaotic overcoat of our daily time-fractured experiences, is far too great to contemplate yet.

Our work, then, becomes a continuous recognizing and releasing (a new definition of R&R!) of our limiting thoughts; of shifting from the wrong mind to the right mind, or from attack to forgiveness. We want to do this because "Herein lies the peace of God" (Intro to the Text). It is only through our own power of decision, to decide with our right mind, that we shorten the time we spend in pain.

After 30+ years with this *Course*, i am still overwhelmed with joy each time i catch a limiting thought and ask for its correction. The incredible peace that i experience as a result of each call for help produces an unspeakable fullness, a eureka! moment, a miracle!

Reader Reflection/Action ~

Set aside a few minutes to practice recognizing a limiting thought—perhaps one you have believed about yourself for a long time. What benefit is there to you holding on to this belief? Are you willing to make the shift to your right mind for correction of this thought? Close your eyes for 3 minutes. Imagine your best friend, who always supports you and loves you unconditionally, is sitting next to you. Tell hir what's on your mind. Then listen to hir advice. What did s/he say?

Lesson 15

My thoughts are images I have made.

It is midwinter as i write these words today yet the thought of weeds has come to mind, probably because the latest snow has melted and i can see the tenacious greens planted by Mother Nature already making their appearance.

From a weed's point of view, getting plucked is a painful experience and usually fatal. It wants to live. It wants to perpetuate itself. This is all it knows how to do. The same can be said for the ego. Our Teacher is leading us firmly—telling us that we must first remove the distractions of ego image-making, the "weeds" that have sent their roots deep into our thinking process, replacing our real thoughts of unconditional love.

I read this lesson and am thunderstruck by the power we possess. We are told that everything we see is based merely on what we are thinking: "It is because the thoughts you think you think appear as images that you do not recognize them as nothing. You think you think them, and so you think you see them . . . This is the function you have given your body's eyes. It is not seeing. It is image making. It takes the place of seeing, replacing vision with illusions." (W15.1)

Woe to the weeds! We study to remember we are the gardener, not the weeds, nor the soil which is helpless in averting undesirable seeds from sprouting in it. We have the right *and the power* to remove the life-sapping weeds, clearing the way for the gorgeous blooms of truth.

This concept of responsibility is in direct contrast to Christianity's doctrine of vicarious salvation through "the blood of Jesus." We are saved, says the *Course*, when we take responsibility by unearthing our limiting thoughts and asking for their correction from the Source. This requires no external savior, no physical structure at all. Merely a change of mind!

This news can be liberating or extremely disconcerting. If reading this lesson makes you feel like a novice in the garden of life, *do not* let that stop you. Remember, that is a fear thought, which cannot be a real thought because it separates you from your peace.

The goal of this *Course* is peace of mind, 24/7. The only way to accomplish your goal is to stick with what you trust. If you have taken up this study, then stay with the practice to its natural conclusion. I have yet to lose trust in this Course. Even though i might not have liked what it has told me in specific cases through the years, i have realized tremendous peace from its teachings, and continue to do so.

Bodies need muscles to do their labor; minds need willingness (spiritual muscles) to succeed in producing a bountiful garden filled with peace. "These exercises will not reveal knowledge to you. But they will prepare the way to it." Knowledge, as the *Course* defines it, is not a compendium of facts. Rather, it is the awareness of our oneness with our Source. It is the achievement of one-mindedness with God. As we work to pluck the weeds of false thoughts from our mind, we move closer to the peace that foreshadows our return to Paradise!

Reader Reflection/Action ~

Do you believe in your personal power to change the things you see, including the limiting thoughts you have? Close your eyes. Maybe immediately, or in a little while, you will begin to see people's faces in your mind's eye, or places, or situations as if they are right in front of you in this moment. See if you can relate this inner experience with what you see when you open your eyes.

Lesson 16

I have no neutral thoughts.

"Thoughts are things and they have wings." Perhaps you've heard this witty aphorism. It implies what today's lesson says: There are no neutral thoughts. How many times have you had a thought and then dismissed it saying, "What does it matter what i think?" or "That's a stupid idea. Forget it." Today's idea gives us pause to think again.

When the separation from our Creator seemed to occur, our mind was split in two and the ego was born, manifesting a world of duality. The principle is simple enough. Our thoughts are powerful enough to give "rise to the perception of a whole world" (2:3) separate from Heaven. "There are no idle thoughts. All thinking produces form at some level." (T2.VI.9:12-13) Because of Who we are, our thoughts are powerful. They have the ability to maintain chaos or bring peace to our mind. Therefore, there is nothing more important than discerning our unreal thoughts. There is no other way to achieve true peace.

Easier said than done. We are entranced by the images we have made and are immensely resistant to relinquishing them. Where would we be without our illusions? "Struck down by God!" the ego warns. And so, we are content to stay in our aberrant world, far away from our vengeful creator. (See Day 13.) Yet, as we study, there is a quiet prompting, an internal nudge that shows us "little edges of light around familiar objects." (L15.2:2) This is *not* to be taken literally although some may experience it so. If you've been studying for 11 years and have never had a "light episode," you are *not* flunking the *Course*! Our Teacher says these light episodes may take many different forms. After all, we are seeing what is not there and as we begin to give our images less value, they will diminish in different ways. An example:

Years ago, i was driving on the Long Island Expressway through Queens to visit my husband at the Hospital for Special Surgery in the city. He had just had his second hip replacement surgery (on the same hip) because he had decided to go rollerblading with our daughter. *Would they be able to repair the damage he had done or would he end up in a wheelchair?* This was how my thoughts were running. Suddenly, i noticed smoke seeping out from the vents on the dashboard. "OMG, something's burning in the engine!" i thought, my heart racing. I was able to pull over to the side of the highway where i began to have a serious meltdown. A million thoughts collided through my mind. I was frantic. "What am i to do?" i wailed internally.

Then somehow (a miracle), out of the deep dark fog (Fear Of God) in my mind, came a new thought: "This is all a product of my frightened mind. Please help me, Jesus, to see this differently." A sense of stillness and peace enveloped me. I took a few slow deep breaths. I heard, "You can go on now. All is well." And it was. Smoke gone, car fine. I had allowed myself to release the image i had made.

Opposites are the natural occurrence in a dualistic system. Several pairs are offered to us today that are used throughout the material. The words on the left represent true thoughts whereas those on the right make up the foundation of the ego realm.

true—false	create—make
extend—project	peace—war
love—fear	real—unreal

The words *make* and *create* have special significance throughout the material. *Make* is most often paired with the ego or wrong mind whereas *create* is reserved for God and the right mind. As I mentioned on Day 14, we will be learning new and specific meanings for words we recognize and have used previously in other ways. This is one of the reasons many people have difficulty reading the *Course* on their own. It is definitely not a novel to be breezed through or a mystery where you read the end first to alleviate the suspense! There is great benefit to reading each sentence deliberately, listening with that internal ear for the deep meaning it has for you.

One of the purposes of the Workbook is to slow our thinking down so that we can grasp our limiting (painful, jealous, anxious, spiteful, giddy) thoughts and see them for what they really are: the ego's attempt to keep the separation fully active. So, when we are asked to look around the room or monitor our thoughts, we are learning how to access our thoughts at a much slower rate than in our typical ego-automatic state. This is the gentle method of a loving Teacher who is offering us a technique and a means of changing our hurtful thoughts so we can get off the rollercoaster and transfer to a smooth gliding sedan on our journey home.

Reader Reflection/Action ~

Can you think of another pair of words that apply to your life? A set of opposites that have been part of your illusions? Spend some quiet time observing your thoughts. See if you can notice how you handle a fearful thought—do you push it away? Do you minimize its importance? Do you look for someone to blame for your fear?

Lesson 17

I see no neutral things.

It may take years to fathom the radical nature of these early lessons. They are calling for a complete reversal of the way we think because we have adopted an ego thought system that was not given to us by our Creator. Our Brother Jesus has come to teach us that everything we believe is true here, is *not*. It is the product of our willful desire to make a world where God cannot enter. This is the sum focus of the ego's system. So, in this world, there are a seemingly endless number of causes and an equally vast number of effects from those causes.

The idea of cause and effect in this lesson is a foundational concept in the material. The *Course* teaches that God is first Cause and we, the Christ, are the Effect. In truth, this is not a dualistic concept because there is no separation between God, Who thinks, and the Christ which is What God thinks. "Thoughts are not born and cannot die. They share the attributes of their creator, nor have they a separate life apart from his. The thoughts you think are in your mind, as you are in the Mind Which thought of you. And so, there are no separate parts in what exists within God's Mind. It is forever One, eternally united and at peace." (T30.III.6:5-9) One Cause and Its Effect—there is need for nothing more.

But, since that simple fact does not satisfy an ego that is constantly seeking more effects, we need to spend much time discovering the multitudinous forms this idea takes. Here we read, "It is always the thought that comes first, despite the temptation to believe it is the other way around." The ego wants to believe that something happens in the world and then we have a thought about it. This is not so. (See Lesson 190.5 for a very clear statement regarding this.)

If i am angry at someone, it is not because of any specific thing s/he has done. We believe we get angry at a person's actions in that moment but, in truth, the anger is already present and steps forth in warranted indignation when it can find a reasonable excuse (see Day 5, I am never upset for the reason i think).

This lesson again makes the point that every thought is either true or false; it will bring peace or dis-ease. No thought is neutral or without effect. We are given the argument that perception always has a cause and is not a cause in itself. In other words, the thought comes first and then we perceive its effects. The justification for the argument is that perception is always shifting and changing so how could it possibly be a true cause? We have courts and judges because someone has to decide which perception is correct, otherwise total chaos would ensue.

Said another way, i see no neutral things because i have no neutral thoughts. Seeing follows thinking and thinking is derived from one of two possible sources in this world: the ego or the right mind. Merely being in this world indicates we have chosen the ego initially as the origin of thought. In doing so, we espouse duality. Then, everything is either good or bad, right or wrong, etc. Neutrality is not an option for the ego. True joy is impossible in this world because joy is total and cannot shift or change.

When our real thoughts become apparent to us we will no longer have sad or happy thoughts, angry or calm thoughts, magnanimous or jealous thoughts. We will have completely reversed our thinking and have only the thoughts we think with God, the thoughts that stem from joy.

Reader Reflection/Action ~

If possible, take a walk today and, as you walk, look around. What happens as your eyes fall upon an object or a person you pass on your way? If you can't take a walk, you can do the same exercise simply by closing your eyes and observing your reaction to your thoughts. Next time you have an angry thought (probably within the hour, if not sooner!), attempt to discern if your anger really stems from your current perception. Can you imagine another cause?

Lesson 18

I am not alone in experiencing the effects of my seeing.

Our lesson today reaffirms that we have no dispassionate thoughts nor are we alone in our thinking. The inference is that our thoughts are important because they determine the world we see. If we are unhappy, it is not because of what we see, it is because of the choice we make each moment to view our reality through the lens of the ego.

We're like magnets that pull toward us that which complements our thoughts. We also draw together with like-minded individuals forming all the myriad groups that exist in the world. These are our lovers and friends in whom we take refuge from a dire world.

A fascinating example of how the ego uses the idea of unity is in what can be called "group think" or the madness of crowds such as mass hysteria. Here, the individual gives up hir autonomy to the collective consciousness of the group. As such they form a blanket of undisputed agreement that excludes anybody who refuses indoctrination. Depending on the group's purpose, the result can be merely exclusionary at one end, or greatly destructive at the other, such as a terrorist organization.

Naturally (to the ego), there are many others who do not think as we do, and so we set them outside our circle of "love." Be it a renegade family member or a mass murderer, this is the formation of a divided world where it seems that there can be another who is unlike us. The ego is delighted and energized to have someone to point a finger at and say, "You are the cause of my unhappiness."

This is the state of affairs in which we see ourself these days. But we (who are *not* the ego), are not pleased, we are anxious, sad, angry, scandalized. We say we want peace and contentment yet all we see is disaster. Still, there are times when we sense that there could be "another way" to look upon our world. It is in these quiet moments when we allow the Voice for God to speak in us whispering gently, "Allow yourself to feel the Peace that God gave you."

I will mention many times throughout the material that as long as we see anyone as different from ourself, we will not have the peace of God. Our ego will tell us to stop reading now because it's obvious that people are different, always have been and always will be. But perhaps there is a nagging doubt that the ego is right.

Reader Reflection/Action ~

Examine your closest friendships—are they merely "birds of a feather," people who reinforce your own ego's ideas? Think about an organization or group that you could join that would stretch your complacent beliefs. If you're a Democrat, attend a Republican group, for example!

Lesson 19

I am not alone in experiencing the effects of my thoughts.

Cause and effect are inseparable, this lesson tells us. Our thoughts are the cause and our seeing is the effect. Or, conversely, we see something and experience something because of the way we think. The simultaneous nature of cause and effect is an important teacher. It can tell us which part of our split mind we are embracing. A scary thought, a disappointment, an angry exchange with someone all indicate we have chosen the ego or wrong mind to be the lens through which we see the world. Realizing that the choice we've made is actually a choice, allows us to make a new decision.

To our egocentric Western mind, today's lesson offers another radical idea: "It is a fact that there are no private thoughts." (L19.3) "Nonsense!" says our ego. "I don't know what s/he is thinking and vice versa." Our ego *knows* this is true because we literally can't get inside one another's brain (unless you're a neurosurgeon). Or can we?

The ego assures us that the space that surrounds our bodies precludes total mental intimacy. So, we are safe from prying minds that might discover what we're really thinking. We shudder at the possibility that our thoughts could be known to others, because our ego thoughts are cause for shame. Since they are always defensive, they are filled with judgment and attack. To ourself, we say things that are not true, to puff ourself up and to make others little. So, it follows that we would not want these thoughts to be known by others. "And they can't be," says the ego, "unless you torture me and force me to reveal them." Torquemada notwithstanding, the ego is incredibly successful at using guilt to wring out confessions. Therefore, are we ever really safe?

To say there are no private thoughts implies that every thought that was ever thought or ever will be thought is already accessible to every thinker. This is a level of equality that is impossible in the ego realm. It completely annihilates the "old souls" idea. If we all know each other's thoughts, then no one is smarter or wiser than the next because we are all continuously being created at once in our Source. In other words, there never was, is, or will be a time when we are not all together as one Son of a wholly loving Creator.

Does the "no private thoughts" concept in our *Course* then require us to perceive one another on a level playing field, without any distinctions whatsoever? Yes and no. (What other answer would you expect from a dualistic mind?!) Kidding aside, it would be "a particularly unworthy form of denial" (T2.IV.3:11) to maintain that there are no differences between bodies and brains in our current state of awareness.

We do not have to defend against what always has been untrue but we *do* need to recognize *what* we believe before we can change it. And we *do* need to determine how well our beliefs are working for us.

The body and its thoughts are the effect of the ego belief system and stand as a unit. From its perception, we *do* see distinctions that range from the horrid to the sublime. Our mostly judgmental thoughts must be sheltered from scrutiny to preserve our autonomy. Our job as *Course* students is to realize our private thoughts are known by everybody on some level. Once we begin to share our thoughts, we are surprised (shocked, pleased) to hear that others have the very same thoughts. Thus, we can see them *without* judgment, with no need to deny them.

Why would we want to deny our differences? Not just because our *Course* tells us to (because *there are no differences*), but because we inherently know something is wrong about the world we experience with our five senses. We want to love and be loved but finding true love seems so elusive. The world is a scary place filled with rogue microbes, crazed killers with big guns, and time that eats away at our bodies and brains. Could all this have been created by a loving God?

As we begin to accept that there are no private thoughts (because all egos have the same thought of the belief in separation in some form), we experience more peace, more happiness (on the way to joy), and less guilt about our no-longer-private thoughts!

Reader Reflection/Action

For as much of the day as possible, catch your unloving thoughts and ask for their correction from the Holy Spirit. How are those around you affected? How does the day transpire differently than yesterday? Then, can you recall an incident when you thought of someone and then the phone rang and that very person was on the line? Or you're talking to a friend and discover you both bought tickets to the same concert or show?

Lesson 20

I am determined to see.

In our ego mind, we are determined to see injustice, evil, fraud, cruelty, deviousness, and deviation. We are determined to feel victimized, to be in bodily pain, to suffer from others' attacks upon us, and to be tortured by our own thoughts. We do not question the validity of any of these ideas because we have the evidence produced by our five senses to justify it. We can touch the painful knee. We can hear the hurtful words. We can smell the fire burning. We can see the destruction of war. As has been mentioned before, we see what we want to see, nothing more and nothing less. We are not victims of the world but of our own belief system. The ego is a harsh master, inflicting the necessary amount of discomfort to maintain the illusion of separation. As long as we choose to see through its eyes, we will continue to suffer. "As you decide so will you see. And all that you see but witnesses to your decision." (T12. VII.11:8-9) This is a universal law of cause and effect.

Cause and effect is a major theme in our study. What we are determined *not* to see is that *all* we see with the body's eyes is simply a reflection of the beliefs in our mind—mental constructs of a split mind. We have chosen to deny our inheritance as God's holy creation, established in love to be only loving, and have accepted instead that we are autonomous egos living in individual forms.

Our power as God's Creation is limitless and thus we have been able to construct a world made of flesh and bone, air and earth, vapor and intensity. We have been hypnotized by the ego belief system to accept only its version of reality. It has related a story of sin and separation to us and convinced us that we *are* that story.

A large part of the problem is that we are unable to tell the difference between misery and happiness. Have you ever loved someone so much that it hurt? Probably. Our egos are masterful at manifesting confusion between apparent opposites. We therefore need to be taught to discern when we are in pain and then decide that it is not joyful. This however, is usually a long and arduous process because of our profound confusion between pain and joy (see T7.X).

Another difficulty we face in learning to see with "new eyes"—what the *Course* calls "vision"—is our heavily undisciplined mind. It is undisciplined in favor of the ego belief system which lionizes helplessness—what i call being on "ego-automatic." It reiterates endlessly how hugely immense is the task of success. "Well, you can try," it counsels, "but it's going to be very hard." So, we often give up when the going gets rough to prove the ego's "truth." And even when we achieve success, its sweetness is short-lived because it is judged successful by the ego which is only concerned with continuously manipulating the physical universe and is never content to rest in peace. There will quickly be another hurdle to jump.

For quite a while i've become aware of the interconnectedness of things from moment to moment in my life. In my classes, it never fails that the meditation will match up with the reading. I'll hear something on the radio or read an article in the newspaper about something i wanted to know about. I'll be talking to a new acquaintance and discover we have friends in common, etc.

So i was not surprised at the interconnectedness of my life and these lessons when i reread today's lesson several years ago, because i was literally dealing with my eyesight. I was diagnosed with wet macular degeneration in 2010 after i noticed a distortion in my left eye. The retinologist said that we caught it in its early stage. Treatment was immediately helpful and i was seeing normally for several weeks when i began to notice distortion again. I received another treatment, an injection in the eye, but this time it didn't help immediately. The distortion was so bad that i had to close my left eye to see the computer screen. My lesson that day was, "I am determined to see." My silent plea for aid produced what i like to call an opportunity to see things differently! My Guide asked me, "Could you choose to be peaceful even if your eyes no longer could see the physical world?" I sat quietly with that question for a while. And soon i knew that i could do anything with my Guide beside (within) me.

Initially we are on ego-automatic. That is why these early lessons show is that we have no real thoughts. All our thoughts stem from the ego and are, by definition, fearful. It is by doing the lessons, while confronting our thoughts head-on, not minimizing, denying, or projecting our thoughts, which gently allows vision to take the place of seeing. This is the invitation to the Holy Spirit, the right part of our mind, where peace reigns, where there are no limiting thoughts that separate us and cause us all the many forms of pain.

And when i said "I am determined to see," i was giving myself the chance to go beyond the seeing of the ego to begin unpacking the fear of blindness that the ego massaged so enthusiastically; to look with "new eyes" on my situation. What i realized was that i was developing trust in the Holy Spirit to guide me through whatever my script presents, to the joy that surrounds me in every moment. With the help of my Guide, i am determined to see the endless peace beyond the chaos of my ego.

Reader Reflection/Action ~

Are you willing to admit that the way you think now could use improvement? And that it is possible for you to make the necessary changes? Let's test your mental discipline today. On the hour, throughout the day, say, "I am determined to see."

Lesson 21

I am determined to see things differently.

If you've been paying attention to the lessons so far, it should be clear that you need to clean up your thoughts. Hopefully the last 20 days have brought us to a level of intimacy with our thoughts that we've never had before. We now begin to realize how many angry, jealous, depressed, anxious, retaliative, judgmental thoughts we have. This is great news! A basic tenet of our study is that we have the power to choose the kind of thoughts we want and, in fact, are doing so continuously. Either they are peace thoughts or attack thoughts, regardless of the form, as those are the only choices we have.

This lesson points out the importance of doing lessons consecutively, as one builds on the work of the last. We are linear thinking creatures, living in the past and projecting into the future and so our Teacher works with us in our present belief system. It also gives a very brief nod to the idea of "special relationships," which is a major construct we will need to address.

To quote miracle principle #1: "There is no order of difficulty in miracles. One is not harder or bigger than another. They are all the same." (T1.1) This applies to all perceptions we experience as well. Therefore, there are no degrees of anger: "a slight twinge of annoyance is nothing but a veil drawn over intense fury." (W21.2:5) Any perceived degree of emotion is meaningless. We only think we understand the reasons for the things we think and do (and sometimes we'll even admit we don't!).

The ego would have us believe that we can love and hate someone at the same time. No way!! Both emotions are false if cohabitation (in the mind) is attempted. These are the kind of thoughts that are false or unreal thoughts. They cover up our real thoughts of love and peace that are available but not selected, like the menu items on your word processing program. We must make a conscious effort to become aware of our thoughts or we will continue on ego-automatic.

We say we want peace. But we must come to realize how much resistance we have to being wrong. We've been told that the world we see with our eyes is the world we have *chosen* to perceive based on our beliefs. So, either we 'fess up and accept that we've been wrong about everything we believe, or we continue to accept our victimhood and let the pain continue unabated. I'd rather be wrong. What about you?

Reader Reflection/Action ~

Re-enact a recent conflict in your mind, but this time remove your attack thoughts and try again. How does it turn out? Building on our discipline exercise of yesterday, three times today, with several hours in between, stop, close your eyes, and seek out any anger thoughts (from mild to intense), then say, "I am determined to see things differently."

Lesson 22

What I see is a form of vengeance.

Recently, i said there are only two thoughts we really have: peace thoughts or attack thoughts. Our ego, having chosen attack, says, "They did it to me. Life isn't fair. Why are they so selfish and inconsiderate?" as it projects these ideas onto others. Now it seems as though these people are attacking us when in truth, we have attacked them. We have conveniently forgotten that we attacked first and now play the victim. "Having projected his anger onto the world, he sees vengeance about to strike at him. His own attack is thus perceived as self-defense." (W22.1.2-3) Ask any guilty prisoner if he did it and he'll answer either that he is innocent or that somebody made him do it. The ego either denies or projects its crimes.

So, today we continue the process of recognizing that our attack thoughts are continuously projected onto the world (our friends, bosses, family members, the supermarket clerk who forgets to put the pickles in our bag, the IRS, the big bankers who stole all our retirement funds, the terrorists, etc., etc.) That is because *we are on ego-automatic*! Unless and until we assume responsibility for our thoughts, we will remain the victim of them.

A word or two about projection. We have Sigmund Freud to thank for the concept of projection. *Wikipedia* defines it as: "a psychological *defense mechanism* where a person unconsciously *denies* his or her own attributes, thoughts, and emotions, which are then ascribed to the outside world, such as to the weather, or to other people. Thus, projection involves imagining or *projecting* the belief that others have those feelings."

Brilliant as he was, Freud wasn't able to take his idea to its farthest limits. He didn't accept that *every* thought the ego mind has is a form of projection, thus we make up the entire world we see. It is no surprise that we walk through our life feeling defensive and frightened. This "savage fantasy" continues to haunt every waking moment until we see its fatal flaw when we choose a miracle instead. The first time we experience this shift in our perception is literally earth-shattering! Now i know it is *me* who chooses to see the sin and keep myself in a prison of pain. And, in that instant, i am free to make the choice for peace. What we are beginning to understand is that our vengeful, angry thoughts hurt only us. When we make a new choice, we leave behind our victimhood.

Reader Reflection/Action ~

Have you ever felt victimized or unfairly attacked? Have you ever been the perpetrator of an attack? Three times today, with several hours in between, glance around at the objects and people nearby. Say to yourself, "Everything i see here will change and is therefore not real. I made these things out of fear. Do i want to keep these fears?"

Lesson 23

I can escape from the world I see by giving up attack thoughts.

Here is a clear statement that affirms i am not a victim but a determiner! "Every thought you have makes up some segment of the world you see. It is with your thoughts, then, that we must work if your perception of the world is to be changed." (W23.1:4)

My thoughts are the cause of my perception, and the world i see and how i see it, is the effect. What my eyes see is not where the problem is . . . it is my *belief* about the world i see that is the problem.

For this reason, there is no point in trying to change the world to make us happy. This doesn't mean that we shouldn't attempt to help people or do good things in the world. It means that we don't expect that what we do will change anything in the world. We do whatever we do because it comes from the guidance we receive from our right mind. Only *changing our thoughts* can make change happen.

Salvation comes when we take back the power of decision in our mind. What we see with the ego are hallucinations, so we want to learn how to see with our right mind where "vision already holds a replacement for everything you think you see now." Saying it another way, we want to peel back the layers of delusion we placed over reality.

Today we are given a very practical formula to accomplish this transformation of our thoughts:

1. Recognize your unreal (painful, angry, sad, etc.) thought. Do not minimize, deny, or project it.
2. Be willing to let it go because to keep it is to remain in pain.
3. If you have followed the first two directions with integrity, you will open the door in your mind to accept a miracle (a change of perception)!

Reader Reflection/Action ~

Two times today, early and late, spend 5 minutes observing your thoughts of being attacked mentally or physically, and of being an attacker. In truth, they are the same although it may take a while to understand this. When you get a clear thought say, "I can break free of the world i see by giving up my attack thoughts about______."

Lesson 24

I do not perceive my own best interests.

This lesson clearly defines *learning* as a process that has barely begun. Our ego is bound to be annoyed when we are told that our perception is completely in error and therefore we cannot know what is best for us. Today's exercises "require more honesty than you are accustomed to using." (W24.3) We are being led carefully back into our mind which is the locus of the thoughts we think. Once there, we can honestly recognize what we are thinking if we are willing to accept that we may have been wrong!

Our Teacher asks us to spend 2 minutes examining a current unresolved concern emphasizing the outcome we would like to have. "You will quickly realize that you have a number of goals in mind as part of the desired outcome, and also that these goals are on different levels *and often conflict.*" (W24.4:3) The reason we do not perceive our own best interests is because we are listening to the ego or the mischievous part of our mind. Like the ancient Greek nature sprites, the ego appears harmless and fetching, but is devious, deranged, and devilishly evil in its actions. It projects and then reacts to what it sees as outside itself as an innocent victim. Under these conditions, it is impossible to know what is best for us. The situation or person we perceive will seem to be attacking us and therefore requiring defense. Thus, the projection/defense mode has been set in motion and cannot be altered without a complete change of mind!

So i took my eye issue as my concern this morning. And lo and behold! There i saw a number of imagined outcomes: 1. I go to the retinologist and he gives me a treatment that cures the distortion. I love this! 2. The retinologist tells me i'm in a holding pattern. Hmm, not the greatest news. 3. He tells me the eye is rapidly deteriorating and i'll be blind soon. This is my real fear. Well, obviously, there is a definite conflict here!

You may well ask how this can be for someone studying this Course for 30+ years. It's a valid question and i answer it this way: The *Course* does not teach that we will have no ego thoughts until that very last moment when we entirely give up the ego belief system: the sudden enlightenment of the Buddhists or resurrection in Christianity. What it does offer is a time collapse, which is the time it takes to access a fear thought and the decision to let it go. Today i can laugh at the crazy, sad, defensive, jealous thoughts of my ego and, by doing so, release their grip on my mind. The lack of importance i give them allows them to fade rapidly away.

As we build our spiritual muscles, we tap into the right mind more frequently and more quickly. The result is a peaceful mind.

Reader Reflection/Action ~

Have you been sabotaged by your ego? Lost something seemingly important because of defensive reactions? Spend 2 minutes three times today examining your mind for unresolved issues. See how many scenarios you devise for each one!

Lesson 25

I do not know what anything is for.

This lesson is a variation on a theme, encouraging you to take a really good look at your thoughts to discover how random, conflicted, and meaningless they are. This self-examination is "not for cowards" as my first Miracles teacher Paul used to say. And, if we're still here, then we must indeed be brave spiritual adventurers! Change is not something the ego encourages. In fact, it will usually put up quite a fight to keep things the way they have been, arguing that what we are familiar with is better than the scary unknown.

What the ego is really afraid of, however, is losing control of our mind. We might, at any moment, decide that the ego is not our friend and turn away from it. This is its greatest concern, and it will do anything to prevent that from happening. So, what the ego does is convince us that our interests are unique to us and must be protected. It is incapable of admitting that all things are for everyone's benefit and no one's interests are different. In other words, that all minds are joined.

We are entering into a realm of new possibilities, but there are impediments to our progress. Our mind is like a hoarder's basement, filled to the brim with old newspapers, broken shards, moldy birdseed and outdated clothes. There is hardly room to turn around, much less put something new in. And, so, we must begin the hard work, physically and emotionally, of removing this ancient junk to open up a space for something new. As long as i think i know what things are for, as long as i hold on to all the old ways i have of perceiving my life, i am reinforcing the pact i've made with the ego which is mired in the past and frightened of the future.

"Purpose is meaning." (W25.1.1) There is much to ponder in these three words. We are being asked, probably for the first time, to discern the purpose of every thought we are able to access in our mind. In so doing, if we are being as honest as possible, we are going to be shocked by its contents: the ancient hatreds, buried fears and doubts, hidden jealousies, and all the personal interests that absorb our mind, 24/7. And because we are on ego-automatic, we think we can have a purpose different from everybody else. Aren't we shocked to hear that we have no personal interests because *we are not the ego?!* What can this mean to an ego? Utter nonsense! Now it begs the question, "If i'm not an ego, then who am i?" Ahhhh, that is the marvelous good news that our *Course* has for us, but not yet . . .. The old junk and cobwebs must first be swept away.

Reader Reflection/Action ~

Six times today, spread out in even time periods, spend 2 minutes gazing about you. As you did in the very first lessons, let your attention rest on various objects randomly. Say, "I do not know what this ____ is for."

Author's Note: Just wanted to mention that i chose the six practice periods as follows: on awakening, before lunch, after lunch, before dinner, after dinner, and at bedtime. It is strongly suggested that you pick specific times for your practice so as to develop your spiritual discipline.

Lesson 26

My attack thoughts are attacking my invulnerability.

Our Teacher is telling us today that we are invulnerable. But this doesn't seem to be possible when we feel so distraught and defenseless. We are given the reason why we feel this way—because we are attacking ourself first, then denying it and finally, projecting it. "Because your attack thoughts will be projected, you will fear attack." (W26.2:1)

At first, we are likely to reject this idea, but if we have been examining our thoughts carefully it will be difficult to maintain the subterfuge. In honesty, we must see how many self-derogatory thoughts are consistently circulating in our mind. The more of them we can catch and correct before they are projected into the world and seen by us in others, the more quickly we can return to a calm and safe mental state. Otherwise we will feel attacked by our projected thoughts and will perpetuate the attack/defense cycle of the ego.

Throughout the material, we are given various metaphysical laws, and today we are being familiarized with one that i'll call the Law of Causation. The world teaches that the people in our life and the situations surrounding them and us are the causes for all our problems. The Law of Causation presents an entirely new explanation for our distress. All problems you perceive begin in your own mind and are then immediately projected outward onto people and things you see in your environment.

In other words, *you are the cause of your problems* and no one else! This is a horrifying yet amazingly freeing thought. If you can relinquish the guilt that arises in accepting your responsibility, then you can celebrate your ability *to change your mind*. You are here to master the *how*! All the lessons are aimed at achieving this goal.

Like a lovely melody heard from a distance, today's lesson gently suggests the thought that we are something much grander than we now currently believe ourself to be. "A false image of yourself has come to take the place of what you are." (3:5) It is these insinuations that keep us striving, moving past our comfort zones, to attempt to discover this elusive "me" that i long to know.

Reader Reflection/Action ~

What is an attack thought you often use against yourself? Your "favorite" way to enhance self-doubt? Spend at least 2 minutes twice today thinking about how you undermine yourself.

Lesson 27

Above all else I want to see.

Here's another crucial concept that is repeated several times in different forms. In Lesson 20 we were "determined to see." It becomes obvious in today's lesson that *seeing* and *vision* are not the same thing. We see a world outside us with our eyes while vision is the internal experience of our True Self.

Today's lesson stresses that *desire is greater than determination*, as anyone trying to diet has encountered. We know what we should do but do we really desire it? If we are holding the ego's hand, then it's a sure bet that we do not. For reasons of its own to be discussed later, the ego is not our friend and does not have our best interests at heart. So, we make plans with all good intentions and then …

Be alert for the unconscious belief that we must sacrifice something valuable in order to "see." Perhaps this is why we have so much trouble remembering this simple statement that we are asked to repeat every half hour. Such frequent application of the idea for the day is quite a departure from the six or less times a day we've been asked so far. This is the first real test we are being given to show us just how undisciplined our mind is (if we haven't already noticed!). Undisciplined or resistant, they are the same.

Our Teacher says that "it will not be difficult" to do this because it is easy to repeat a short sentence to ourself while engaged in other activities. We know this is true because we are continuously having a private conversation with ourself wherever we may be and whatever we may be doing. We are constantly assessing, comparing, judging, rejecting all sensory data that we perceive.

So, the question is not, "How difficult is this?" but, "How much do i want it?" Do i want to see the peace, joy, harmony, camaraderie that is present in in my every encounter throughout the day? Or, do i want to maintain my specialness and all the ego dogma that informs it? Choosing the first is to choose the vision of oneness which sees only peace, while choosing the second strengthens our acceptance of guilt and sacrifice as the norm, thereby maintaining separation.
From Abraham and Isaac to the Holocaust, and beyond into all the daily sacrifices we endure, the ego teaches us that sacrifice is necessary. And we believe it! "No pain, no gain," right? Have we ever stopped to ask "Why?" Why must we suffer to learn? What story did the ego whisper in our ear to convince us of this so-called truth?

For those of us in the West, the story of Adam and Eve's sin against God has infiltrated every thread of our societal fabric. Collectively, we've been born with a black mark already on our soul and seem to need the rest of our life to clean it up. Then, if we do a good enough job, we'll gain a pass into heaven. Unfortunately, Murphy's Law rules supreme. What might go wrong, will go wrong. We try to be good, but there are forces beyond our control that stop our positive progress in its tracks. So, we make more sacrifices, and the suffering continues unabated.

Heaven is a faraway dream.

Suffering only prolongs and promotes itself. The *Course* says we do not need to suffer in order to learn. The vision we are working to achieve will not deprive us of anything. Rather, it will bring blessings, unity, and peace to our troubled mind. Our ego hears this and mutters, "He must be talking to somebody else." We are wanderers, in search of a miracle. At last, we've come to the right place: the holy vision in our right mind!

Reader Reflection/Action ~

See if you can remember the words of this lesson every half hour today. Twice today, upon arising and at the end of the day, think of a time your determination did not match your desire. Notice the guilt feelings that come up. Remind yourself that guilt is merely a thought that manifests in a separated mind, and that you can choose to relinquish it!

Lesson 28

Above all else I want to see things differently.

By adding two words to yesterday's lesson, we add a whole new dimension to the act of seeing. In order to see, we must develop a different perspective. This makes complete sense since we can hardly expect to have a different experience of a situation that we have previously judged as being a certain way. Only a new way of looking at the situation can bring the longed-for peace we desire.

Now we consciously take a stand. Hearkening back to Lesson 25, "I do not know what anything is for," we are willing (hopefully) to entertain the thought that just maybe we don't understand the people and things we see around us as clearly as we thought we did. As unsettling as this idea may seem, it opens up a whole new array of possibilities as to how we see our surroundings and what we believe they are for. These can actually bring us relief!

Because we see separate, individual things, our Teacher says we are not really seeing. The seeing we are attempting to achieve can also be referred to as vision—a way of seeing everything as part of one dynamic wholeness. The right mind does not see separate things. It sees everything in this world in one of two ways: either as coming from love, or in need of love. Either way, the response is always love.

We are able to see things only in these two ways when we give up our past associations with the person or object in front of us. Being fully present in the moment frees us from the tyranny of our judgment which is based in the past, and projected into the future. In that instant, we refuse to accept any new interpretation.

With this lesson we are freeing up space in our mind to allow a new awareness of everyone and everything we perceive. We are making room for a new perspective in the way we view our world. We want to do this because we realize that the way we have looked at people and things in the past has kept us in the hell of "specialness", a state of being that maintains our acceptance of autonomy and suffering. Specialness is the crowning principle of the ego thought system. Our belief in our specialness has the ego's most desired effect—it keeps us separate from one another.

Just one sincere attempt to relinquish a long-held belief will bring great benefits. As we let go of our previously unexamined beliefs about ourself and others (which are steeped in fear and limitation), life becomes a marvelous, enriching experience where everyone and everything is no longer an "other," but a beloved part of us.

The importance of this work cannot be underestimated. We are slowly, gently learning how to hear a different voice. The "raucous shrieking" of our ego is wearing thin, even if it is just a bit! We are actively seeking the real purpose of what we perceive. The ego's goal is to keep us separate and defensive, while this tender new Voice we are beginning to acknowledge has the goal of offering us the very practical gift of a tranquil mind.

Reader Reflection/Action ~

Two times today, discern a long-held belief of yours. Imagine your belief is a deflated balloon. You pick it up and begin to blow into it. As the balloon expands, you are able to see your belief expanding, too. It may even grow into something completely new!

Lesson 29

God is in everything I see.

The first sentence in today's lesson is a showstopper! Our goal is to see "all purpose in everything"; and "to look upon all things with love, appreciation and open-mindedness." Apprehending the meaning of these words is the beginning of our flight from fear. That God is in everything i see is the "whole basis for vision." (W29.1:5) All the previous lessons can be explained by this one simple truth. By choosing to see God (or goodness) all around us, we are choosing correction instead of division.

Obviously, this runs counter to what the ego teaches; each person, place, or thing has a different purpose depending on specific circumstances, and many are seen as aggressively against us. In its anxiety, the ego sees only with suspicion and doubt. "The ego is . . . capable of suspiciousness at best and viciousness at worst. That is its range." (T9VII.3:7)

Now we begin to understand why we're being tested, not cruelly like Job, but intellectually challenged to find the truth. After all, this is a *course* of study, so we should expect our ideas to be tested. We've been asked tantalizing questions and offered suggestive arguments that are rattling the core of our beliefs. Our Teacher entreats us to scrutinize our individual thoughts, as never before, so that we can discern which are useful and which are not. Perhaps, and this is no surprise, we are shocked at how many disjointed, dissolute, detrimental thoughts we have!

Carry on! This is brave work, healing work, enlightening work! Don't look back (you know what happened to Lot's wife!) despite the ego's attempts at heaping guilt on you. Remember Lesson 7, which asserts that our ego sees only the past. We don't want to live in the past anymore! We want to release the past by keeping our attention, breath, and body in this moment.

It is lessons like these and many others we will study that affirm for me, as no other religion or discipline has done, that God is a good, loving Creator Who created us All in love, for only good. It is we who turn our backs on that love when we listen to the ego. So, we take up this study so we can learn how to change our mind and think once again with joy and creativity!

Reader Reflection/Action ~

Six times today, in your predetermined time slots, stop, and looking around, say to whatever your eyes happen to light upon, "God is in this ___." Make every effort not to judge how you feel about certain objects (or people!) as opposed to others.

Lesson 30

God is in everything I see because God is in my mind.

Are we to take this lesson literally? God is in my mind? Sounds heretical! Actually, this is an example of just how different ACIM is from Christianity. Many have claimed this is a quasi-Christian discipline like that of Mormons or Quakers. However, even a cursory study would discover this is so only in form. As i've said previously, many of the words and concepts come from a Judeo/Christian lexicon but they are given completely new meanings in the *Course*. Atonement, Second Coming, Holy Spirit, etc. are some of the words we think we understand from our religious background. This is why it is so important to do what the *Course* asks us: "clear your mind of all past associations . . . to realize how little you understand about them. (W3.2)

The word *mind* is another of the words we think we comprehend. Yet the *Course* makes it clear that the mind is *not* the brain: "You also believe the body's brain can think . . .." (W92.2). All the early lessons are attempting to help us break the shell of belief in the body–brain continuum. We *have* a body and a brain temporarily, until we no longer value them, but we are *not* a body or a brain.

On the other hand, we *do* have a mind that thinks with God, its Source. This is the right mind we are being asked to actuate, to choose instead of the ego mind. Because we are on ego-automatic, we must make a *conscious* decision for the right mind. Not an easy job! As my teacher Paul used to say, "Simple, but not easy."

Perception separates, vision joins. When we know that God, rather than the ego, is in our mind, we will embrace all that we see around us instead of judging, quantifying, and alienating others. *Vision* is another word the *Course* uses differently. It is usually not synonymous with eyesight. Sight is a product of the ego whereas vision is the choice for the right mind.

"Real vision is not only unlimited by space and distance, but it does not depend on the body's eyes at all. The mind is its only source." (W30.5) Today's comparison of vision and perception also notes that space and time are understood in diametrically opposed ways. The ego sees with the body's eyes and is therefore limited in its perception. Thus, it believes that if a person dies s/he can no longer be "seen." Time and distance are irrelevant to vision. People we think about, whether in or out of the body, remain forever in our minds even though we cannot "see" them. Vision is awareness that reaches far beyond any physical constraint.

Reader Reflection/Action ~

As often as possible today, repeat the day's idea as broadly as you can. Spend 2 or 3 minutes twice today considering which of your thoughts you are thinking with God.

Lesson 31

I am not a victim of the world I see.

"Today's idea is the introduction to your declaration of release." When i first saw these words some 30+ years ago, i felt a jolt of freedom, of tremendous relief, of scary possibilities. I wasn't exactly sure what it meant but it had a forthrightness and certainty about it that i wanted more of.

I had never consciously felt myself a victim of the world but i certainly felt put upon by many aspects and people in my life. That is one of the ploys the ego is excellent at utilizing: breaking up the problem so that it seems to be many different problems, external to us, that keep us endlessly busy trying to fix.

I had never been taught, "The inner is the cause of the outer," in school or anywhere else. There was not an inkling of an idea that my problems might originate within my own thoughts. This novel idea caught my imagination so strongly that it became one of my favorite lessons. I am not the victim of the world but, rather, its creator! My world is the result of my thoughts. "Far out!" as they used to say, or "Way in!" as i say today.

Reader Reflection/Action

As often as possible today, affirm, "I am not a victim of the world."

Author's Note: I haven't spent much time discussing the method of training we are receiving, so this lesson is a good place to make mention. We are given two forms of practice. The first we are familiar with from the previous lessons—taking a minute or two to apply the lesson in conjunction with our thoughts as we look about.

The new phase of practice now includes the usage of the lesson frequently throughout the day. It is easy to see how beneficial it is to say, "I am not the victim of the world i see" each time we are confronted with what we perceive as a difficult issue. By affirming these words, we are allowing ourself the opportunity to see the situation in a different light. This takes the lesson from theoretical to practical. It takes the problem from being in the world to being in our mind—how grand and how life-changing!

Lesson 32

I have invented the world I see.

Our lesson today minces no words; clear as a bell, we are told we invented the world we see and see it only because we want to see it! Every so often our Teacher becomes hard-nosed with us. It's appropriate because we lack discipline and need a nudge sometimes to keep us on the straight and narrow. Clarity is also useful. It disallows interpretation and obfuscation which the ego loves to use to keep us uncertain.

The other side of the same coin is that we will not see what we don't want to see. This is a double-edged sword. The ego will not see anything that reduces its anxiety. It does not want peace and will try to shut out whatever attempts we make to remain sure and calm. Its goal is to convince us that we are in imminent danger and must listen to its "guidance" to be saved.

However, our right mind will not see the attempt at separation and will immediately repair any faulty perception. One time, in my yoga class, several members were complaining about how dirty the floor was, acting disgusted. Linda, our yoga teacher, laughed at hearing their complaints. "You should have seen the floor in the H.S. cafeteria where i taught last night. I had pretzel and potato chip crumbs, and juice on my feet!" She chuckled and continued on with the class. The devil is in the details only if we invite him in!

There are numerous levels to understanding what this lesson teaches. For now, we are asked to apply the idea to any disturbance we encounter by saying, "I have invented this situation *as i see it.*" Do not be concerned with the issue of whether you invented the floor, the walls, or the people involved in the situation. Focus only on your *judgment* of the situation. It is our judgments of the occurrences in our lives that cause us grief and therefore are where the *Course* wants us to put our efforts in these early stages. When we take responsibility for our judgments, in other words, when we can say, "i have invented this situation," we *open* ourself to the miracle. As long as we remain a victim of the world we see, peace is not possible.

Reader Reflection/Action ~

Twice today, morning and evening, consider this: the world your ego invented is like a security blanket—taking it away seems scary. What scares you most about admitting you created the problems/strife/drama you face in life? As is the routine now, repeat this idea as often as possible as you go about your day.

Lesson 33

There is another way of looking at the world.

These are hated words to the ego. No self-respecting ego wants to be told that its ideas or beliefs are wrong. Our egos have invested a lot of time in fabricating an elegant scheme in which they play the hero-victim in a world of subtle and covert attackers bent on their destruction. "The ego does not love you. It is unaware of what you are, and wholly mistrustful of everything it perceives because its perceptions are so shifting. The ego is therefore capable of suspiciousness at best and viciousness at worst. That is its range. It cannot exceed it because of its uncertainty. And it can never go beyond it because it can never *be* certain." (T9Vll.3)

So, when we read today that "you can shift your perception of the world in both its outer and inner aspects" (W1.1), it must mean that we are something besides the ego. This is another reference to the split mind i've mentioned before. The whole thrust of our study is to help us strengthen our desire and ability to shift our awareness from the ego to the right mind as quickly as possible.

The point is made again today that our inner and outer observations are the same. It is probably easier to accept that your inner perceptions could be altered since we've been doing the lessons and spending time slowing down the thought process to be able to see our individual thoughts. Now we've noticed how conflicted and confused they truly are.

It may be more difficult to grasp the truth of this lesson regarding our outer perceptions, or how we see the world around us. Consider how many of our unpleasant interactions play out the same way over and over. Try an experiment the next time your special one says the words that will certainly evoke the "prerecorded" response in you that always ends up in a fight. *Stop!* See the dance as an observer and change the music. Respond in a completely different way (be aggressive if you were passive, be sweet if you were mean, and see what happens). "Change but your mind on what you want to see, and all the world must change accordingly." (W132.5)

This suggestion is not as easy as it sounds—you need to really want to change! I do this regularly and am always delighted at the result. It proves to me, in a very powerful way, how tenuous and malleable this world and all our relationships truly are. I'd love to hear from anyone who tries this to know how it went.

One of the metaphors (and there are many) we are given by our Teacher is: the inner and outer worlds we experience are like a play in which we are the writer, producer, director, *and* all the actors! Imagine if we really knew this was true. Consulting with the Holy Spirit, we could then change the script, the various characters, and the plot so that unity and harmony become the context of our play, with miracles as a common occurrence. In fact, this is exactly what we can be doing. We can take this existence and let it be transformed simply by the expression of our will, which is one with God's.

Reader Reflection/Action ~

Have fun today in your reflection time in the morning. Sit with your eyes closed and write yourself a script for the day: who you'll see, what you and others will say, and what will happen. In the evening, review your day. How does it compare to the script you wrote this morning? Any similarities? As usual, repeat the idea throughout the day.

Lesson 34

I could see peace instead of this.

Well, it happened again! I closed the laptop without saving the draft that i'd been working on for almost an hour this morning. Of course, it was the cat's fault—she started knocking things off the table. This is her way of demanding that i play with her. That was my ego's first line of defense. Then i heard, "How could you be so dumb? You know you have to save a draft before closing." "Yes," i said, "but i thought it had auto saved," said the ego. A victim yet again!

Obviously i still hadn't learned the lesson! However, this time i only spent 3 minutes bemoaning my fate. In the past i might have given up on the writing altogether or spent days trying to recoup what i had lost. Then i laughed and thought, "Who cares?" Words can always be replaced; peace cannot. Why should i give up another moment of my precious peace? A sudden flood of relief washed over me. I felt a warmth, a sense of being loved, of safety and acceptance. "I will go out to my gathering of friends and when i return i will complete the lesson."

I am back and want to make two points about today's lesson. My decision to choose peace this morning allowed me to enjoy the day's activity to its fullest. I didn't even think about the writing until we got in the car to come home. "It is from your peace of mind that a peaceful perception of the world arises." (W34.1:4) Had i not let my anger go, i would have spent a good deal of time being anxious and not being present in the moment.

We are told to repeat today's idea frequently "to protect yourself from temptation throughout the day." Here is another example of a recognized word with a very different usage. What temptation would this lesson help us avoid? Eating chocolate cake? If we think of temptation as something that is not good for us we would be right. Anything that does not engender a peaceful mind is going to cause pain and therefore is not good for us. In other words, this lesson saves us from the temptation of accepting the ego's perception of the world. Each time we can catch an ego thought and "choose peace instead of this," we have forsworn temptation!

Reader Reflection/Action ~

Try to count how many times you catch an ego thought and ask for its correction—track your success! As always, take this idea into your day and apply it as often as you can.

Lesson 35

My mind is part of God's. I am very holy.

My eyes almost popped out of my head when i read this lesson the first time! No one anywhere, at home, at my church, or school had ever hinted at the possibility of holiness for themselves or me. Surely this *Course* was like nothing i had ever encountered! "The idea for today presents a very different view of yourself." (W35.3) That's a whopping understatement! We are being told our vision (whatever that may be!) will show us our holiness.

The reason we don't see ourself as holy is a complex story. I gave you a brief summary of the story at the beginning of this book. It begs the question, "How did we get here?" As we read, we gather bits and pieces of the story as we go along. Nowhere in the material is the Origin Story laid out in a unified linear fashion. My teacher Kenneth Wapnick, PhD, has done the most intensive and thorough study and explication of the story. It can be found at www.facim.org in all the material he has published.

This lesson says that we are in this world because we want to be. "You surround yourself with the environment you want." And, certainly here, holiness seems to be in very short supply. We're altering our practice periods today. Now instead of watching our thoughts about the world we see, we are going to study our own self-appraisal! Oh, the novel things our Teacher asks us to do! It would never have occurred to me to make as full and complete a list of my attributes, good and bad, as i possibly could. The ego's whole thrust is on "What do others think of me?" not "Who do i think i am?"

You may find yourself saying, "Well, i thought i was ______. But now i see that i'm beginning to let go of that persona. I don't have to continue to be the angry, disappointed, unappreciated self i seemed to be. With the Holy Spirit by my side, i am expanding my perception of myself to include a whole new creative and caring being who greets each day with happy anticipation of the great things to come!"

Yes, this exercise can be quite an eye-opener if done sincerely.

Reader Reflection/Action ~

Were you taught only God is holy? Does this new understanding of yourself feel comfortable? Three times today, think of as many characteristics, abilities, and prejudices you have about yourself! Write them down in your notebook. Keep in mind that all of them, good and bad, are part of a false self you have manifested as a means of hiding from your holiness. This, i know, is not easy work. But you can do this!

Lesson 36

My holiness envelopes everything I see.

The ego (or wrong mind) lionizes health in a body because it made the body and its chaotic environment. Its goal is always, despite appearances, to keep all things separate. It accomplishes this by insinuating thoughts of doubt, anxiety, fear, defensiveness, jealousy, etc. into all relationships. Remember the ego's range is from suspiciousness to viciousness! It would never allow ideas of holiness to take root and grow.

The right mind is joyously healthy in its thoughts. True health exists only in the mind. Today's lesson is spiritual medicine. It is the antidote for all ego thinking. It immediately shifts the focus from all the ways of maintaining separation to calmness and unity. The *Course* often uses the metaphor of light for true awareness. So, choosing to see holiness in yourself and others instead of the evidence of the ego is like going from a dark room into a sunny day.

Along with spiritual medicine, we need to perform spiritual exercise. Wanting holiness and accepting holiness in your mind are two different levels of thought. Wanting suggests not having whereas accepting is acknowledging ownership.

How do we get from one state to the other? By building our spiritual muscles! The process is the opposite of building bodily muscles. Instead of building up, we want to remove all the layers of defense that hide our holiness from us. Vigilance of thought is the mental exercise required. That is why our Teacher spends so much time in these early lessons on the importance of accessing our thoughts.

In our mindless state, we are on ego-automatic. In this state of consciousness, there is little self-reflection, and the little there is takes the form of self-flagellation and negativity. "Why did i say that? Now i'll lose my job, my friend, my spouse, etc." And, hooray! the ego wins again by cleverly confusing illusions for truth.

In this world, there are all manner of levels and degrees of everything. But in spirit there are none. You are merely sinless. You cannot be a little sinful, or a little happy or a little angry. At any given moment, we are choosing which voice we want to hear and this will determine our state of mind. The miracle occurs when we become aware of an ego thought and ask for correction. Peace is the result, although it may take many different forms until we no longer have a need for form.

Reader Reflection/Action ~

Let's continue to build our spiritual muscles by observing our thoughts! At your regularly assigned times, state today's lesson to yourself and then search your mind for all the "junk" thoughts that keep the truth of your holiness from your awareness. Write them down in your notebook.

Lesson 37

My holiness blesses the world.

Important ideas are often strengthened by shining a light on them from different directions. This is our third day on the theme of personal holiness. For most first-time readers, the idea of being holy is almost sacrilegious. "Who am i to think i'm so wonderful?" says the ego. Yet our Teacher is telling us here that "our purpose is to see the world through your own holiness. Thus, are you and the world blessed together . . . everyone gains through your holy vision." (W37.1:4)

Something very interesting happens in this lesson—something easy to miss on your initial reading. First, the issue of sacrifice is raised. *The word does not come up again until Lesson 100.* Sacrifice is a major tool of the ego. The whole premise of the ego is that sacrifice is necessary in order to accomplish its goal. Nothing comes easy for the ego—pain and suffering are standard fare in its experience. It takes our God given power and turns it against us, like a cancer that eats away at its host.

The ego gave up Heaven to make a world of its own—the greatest forfeit of all!! And once here, it continues to promote sacrifice in all the daily multitudinous thoughts we have of anger, jealousy, disappointment, feelings of failure, being unloved and unappreciated, etc., etc. Thus, it continuously props up the "reality" of the world and all of the people and things in it.

The second interesting occurrence begins in the third sentence, "the perceiver will lose. Nor will he have any idea why he is losing. Yet is his wholeness restored to his awareness through your vision." Who is the perceiver? Your ego! And whose vision restores wholeness? Your vision! Our Teacher is speaking to a "you" that is other than the ego!! My teacher Ken has dubbed this aspect of ourself as The Chooser.

I make this point because it is only the ego that must learn that peace is a blessing and not a curse ("Rest in Peace," it says on the tombstone). Spirit, which is what we are and always have been, does not need to learn anything. Yet, until we accept our True Identity as spirit, we will see a world of duality that will mire us in sacrifice and suffering.

Reader Reflection/Action ~

Have you ever felt blessed by someone else's holiness? Know that you conferred holiness upon this other to avoid seeing it in yourself. Notice, in your practice times, the many judgments you make of the people and things you see or simply think about in your day. With each one, affirm how your holiness blesses it/hir/them.

Lesson 38

There is nothing my holiness cannot do.

The implications of this lesson go far beyond anything our ego can fathom. In fact, the ego is horrified by what this lesson suggests because it negates its belief in being a victim of the world. If there is nothing our holiness cannot do, then there is nothing to be afraid of and nothing we need to defend ourself against.

In other words, this statement is a death knell for the ego! As we begin to take back the power we gave away to the ego, we build our spiritual muscles. The ego begins to lose its sharp-clawed grasp on our thinking, freeing the thoughts of peace and unity that are already there, waiting to be acknowledged.

We know this is occurring when we start to recognize miracles are happening in our daily activities! We become understanding, patient, tolerant. What upset us before suddenly seems trifling, not worth flustering our feathers. We reach for the phone and it rings with the person we wanted to talk to already on the line! We have a desire for a particular thing and then we "coincidentally" come across it the next day. The forms are endless but the content is always some form of peace.

Owning our holiness cannot happen in a vacuum. Holiness is an all-encompassing state of being. If i am holy, then you are holy and so is everything we see. When we see everything with the vision of holiness, there is no space for fear or anger or anxiety.

As our acceptance of our holiness increases, the problems that seemed insurmountable become every day activities like taking out the garbage or buying groceries when the fridge is empty. They need doing and so we do them. Joy becomes our companion in all that we think, say, and do.

Of course, the ego will not tolerate this holiness business for very long! It will attack with all its force to get you back on its track. It will bring you sickness and disaster to tempt you into its trap. But because there is nothing your holiness cannot do, you will notice this intrusion into your peace and demand it step aside as your gaze rests on the Light ahead.

Reader Reflection/Action ~

Is your ego still putting up blocks to peace at this point in your lessons? Of course it is! To deny your experience is only to prolong the pain. We want to be better than the FBI at locating an ego thought and bringing it to our right mind for correction. Today let's see if we can notice the "synchronicities," the unexpected delights, the happy moments we have with others as we go about our activities. Know that these miraculous moments are your just reward for being holy!

Lesson 39

My holiness is my salvation.

Thinking back to my early days with the Workbook, i can remember spending quite a bit of time wondering who these people Helen and Bill were and how this material came to be written. I felt a little jealous that they got to be the "Bringers of the Light." After experiencing a lesson like today's, i soon lost all interest in the who or how, because it was clear to me that their Source was not of this world.

The question today is, if guilt is hell, what is its opposite? This is the first mention in the Workbook of the major idea of guilt, a cornerstone of the ego. I know it was true for me. My mind went blank when asked this question. The answer is too simple! Look at the lesson—it is obvious the answer is, "my holiness." But the ego hates simple answers and always looks to complicate matters. "We are dealing only in the very obvious, which has been overlooked in the clouds of complexity in which you think you think." (W39.1:4)

Alternatively, our Teacher suggests that perhaps we don't consider guilt to be hellish. I know this to be a fact because i've had many conversations with non-ACIMers who say that guilt is necessary and useful to keep us from getting into trouble. The belief is that if we didn't feel guilty for doing "bad" things, we would be out of control and all mayhem would break loose! If we were only egos that would be true, however, because we are spirit in truth, all the beliefs of the ego thought system lack validity.

How do we reveal our holiness? By searching out our unloving thoughts in all their countless forms. Remember, you have unloving thoughts about yourself as well as others. These are often difficult to discern. We need our holiness to save us from our guilty, fearful, self-hating ego thoughts.

Our holiness precludes any need for guilt. Our holiness encompasses not just ourself, but every being that ever was or will be, simply because there is nothing outside of God. As this truth dawns on the mind, it becomes still, at peace, immersed in its holiness.

Reader Reflection/Action ~

At your normal, appointed times today, search your mind for any guilty thoughts. Can you identify how many of the things you do that are motivated by guilt?

Lesson 40

I am blessed as a Son of God.

Okay, students! Today we're having a quiz that will be worth 15% of your final grade. Just kidding! Yet today we are being strongly encouraged to meet the ego at every chalk mark and swipe it off the blackboard. Every 10 minutes of every hour of the 15+ active hours of our learning journey through this day we are to remember and affirm who we are as a Son of God.

Traditionally, in Christian dogma, Jesus was and is the *only* Son of God. So here is another example of the radical nature of this study. We are being taught that *we* are the Son of God, right alongside Jesus! "Awe should be reserved for revelation . . . It is therefore, an inappropriate reaction to me. An elder brother is entitled to respect for his greater experience, and obedience for his greater wisdom. He is also entitled to love, because he is a brother . . . It is only my devotion that entitles me to yours. There is nothing about me that you cannot attain." (T1.II.3) Wow! Jesus is saying that he is our older brother, therefore we are equal to him in every way, except in time! We have yet to achieve his wisdom. But we can and will!

Consider the way the ego works in the world. While we are having a conversation with anyone, there is a little voice we hear in our head commenting on (judging) this person and what s/he is saying. In other words, there are two conversations going on simultaneously—one externally with the other person and another internally within our own mind.

Now imagine you are doing Lesson 40 for the day. You know you must try to repeat the lesson at least every 10 minutes. So here you are, talking to this other person, making your assessments and you suddenly remember to say your lesson, "I am blessed as a Son of God." While you are saying this lesson and conversing with this person, *there is no judgment*. You cannot be affirming your true Identity and judging at the same time! In fact, you may experience a shift in perception (a miracle!) where you see no separation between you and the other person!

In a nutshell, this is the purpose of these lessons: to stop the judgments of the ego and replace them with the loving acceptance of the right mind. You might be saying, "Oh, but i can't let people take advantage of me—i must be able to recognize where they are coming from."

These doubts will deter you in your ability to remember the lesson as frequently as requested by our Teacher. However, *do not* let this be an opportunity for your ego to say, "See, you can't do this *Course*! It's too hard!" Our Teacher's principle tool is forgiveness, and this situation is the perfect place to relinquish guilt by forgiving *yourself!*

When we get the ego out of the way, in other words, when we accept Who We Are, our right mind will be free to discern what to do or say to effectuate a healing outcome for all. And it will do it without attacking (as the ego would do) because it sees its purpose in complete alignment with everyone else. Herein lies the peace of God, the goal of our study!

Reader Reflection/Action ~

So here is a true test of your discipline (or lack thereof!). Can you traverse your day with 10-minute insertions of light, peace, and joy? Can you state with certainty how blessed you are? Again, this is not an attempt to heap guilt upon yourself if you forget to affirm Who you are. But it is a reality check that says, "There's more work to do." Don't give up!

Lesson 41

God goes with me wherever I go.

Overwhelmed by the beauty of today's lesson, let me quote its heart: "Today's idea will eventually overcome completely the sense of loneliness and abandonment all the separated ones experience. Depression is an inevitable consequence of separation. So are anxiety, worry, a deep sense of helplessness, misery, suffering and intense fear of loss." (W41.1)

So, we are miserable without God. Our ego would not admit this. On the contrary, it will convince us that we are perfectly happy except for . . . this one little problem. What our ego doesn't want us to remember is that it made up the problem, and keeps making up new problems, to keep us from revitalizing our True Identity, as this would be its demise.

The ego would have us believe that God is somewhere else or nowhere at all. The ego would have us believe that we have many problems to which it has the answers if we just wait long enough. And we do (because we are on ego-automatic), until we ask a real question. Instead of wanting to know how to get so-and-so to change hir mind, i might rather choose to know *why* i'd want to change hir mind. If we are asking sincerely, we might be very surprised at the answer we receive.

This *Course* is a remedy for our apparent separation from our Source. "Deep within you is everything that is perfect, ready to radiate through you and out into the world. It will cure all sorrow and pain and fear and loss because it will heal the mind that thought these things were real, and suffered out of its allegiance to them." (W41.3)

"Not so fast," says the ego. "How do you know you can trust this Pollyanna program that wants you to think you're so great?!" And so, we curl into our feathers and go back to sleep. The proof that we refuse to doubt the ego can be clearly seen in how well we did with yesterday's lesson. If you didn't remember to say, "I am blessed as a Son of God," every 10 minutes throughout the day, it is not because you are stupid or forgetful. It is merely the ego's resistance to the truth. It will fight to its last breath to keep you from remembering your holiness and the "unfailing companionship" and protection that surround you.

Reader Reflection/Action ~

Let's take a break today. If you'vc been reading these lessons consecutively, you've taken in more Truth and Love than in the whole rest of your life! You are beginning to realize you are not alone in the universe. There is a loving Presence that accompanies you everywhere you go. It would not be surprising if you still had moments of doubt—Rome wasn't built in a day and your spiritual muscles are still flabby!

However, if you want to keep moving forward, take time at least in the morning and evening to affirm that you are never alone-God goes with you everywhere.

Lesson 42

God is my Strength. Vision is His Gift.

As a new student of the *Course* in the early 1980s, i heard many divergent views of the material. This was a time when several cult groups became notorious for their harmful practices. One opinion i heard circulating about the *Course* was that it was a form of brainwashing, an allusion to cultic activity. I thought about this first with alarm but then with mirth. If this is brainwashing, then *i want it*! I long to know that God is my strength and vision is His gift to me. What could be more wonderful to know above all else?

We are *already* brainwashed by the ego into believing that we are alone and full of sin; that we must rely on our own puny strength. Fear is instilled in us because, according to our ego, everybody else is out to take something away from us at the least, and do us in at the worst. We are brainwashed to believe that we live in a world of danger and limitation and must constantly be on our guard for external attacks. I often think that our preoccupation with sports and gym memberships stems from this need to keep in "fighting condition." We accept pain and suffering as necessary inconveniences. No pain, no gain, right?

We are brainwashed by the ego to accept that we are sinners who must pay for our crimes against God (remember Adam and Eve?). We have injured God and need to stay far away from his wrath. This is the birth of fear and guilt into our holy mind; fear that He will find and punish us, and guilt that we are bad and not worth saving. This shows up often in our intense fear of illness and death. As a result of these beliefs, everything and everybody we see is steeped in defensiveness and mistrust.

When we know that God is our strength, all fear disappears. We come to understand that real strength is not having big muscles but a big heart. Real strength empowers us to carry out the instructions of our right mind whose only will is for true justice stemming from love. We move through our day always listening, assured that we will be told exactly what to do, how to do it, and when. We know that God is our loving Creator, not our judge and jury.

To remember God is to embrace His gift of vision. With vision, we see beyond the body's limited view, which is based on maintaining separation. We see the light in ourself and in all God's creation, every individual, not as they see themselves but as we know them to be in truth. Vision brings solutions that fear and judgment could never see.

Reader Reflection/Action ~

What does strength mean to you? Be as honest as possible in your quiet times today. How would you exhibit your strength? Can you see how vision and strength are connected? The only wrong answer is a dishonest one! Remember, if our thinking was on target, we wouldn't need to be doing these lessons.

Lesson 43

God is my Source. I cannot see apart from Him.

Today is a glorious day—we meet the Holy Spirit formally for the first time in the lessons! This is another one of those terms that is given an entirely different meaning than the one you probably know. In this teaching, the Holy Spirit is the *mediator between us and God*. S/he is our Guide, the bridge from the unreal to the real, The Way Shower, Light Bringer, our confidante, and Best Friend. S/he resides in our right mind (which is *not* the brain) which has never separated from the Source. It is only with the Holy Spirit's help that we can overcome our fascination with the ego and return our mind to its reality as spirit.

God doesn't know all the pain and suffering we are experiencing in this dreamworld we made and now seem to inhabit because S/He didn't create it. We made this dreamworld so that we could hide our guilt from view. (Refer to the Creation Story at the end of this book.)

An essential concept of our *Course* is that our mind seems to be split between truth and illusion, between the right mind where the Holy Spirit resides, and the ego or wrong mind.

The Holy Spirit resides in our right mind (it is not a bird or a spirit floating around!). If there were an opposite to the ego, it would be the Holy Spirit. There is a wrong mind (ego) and a right mind (Holy Spirit) as long as we *seem* to be having this ego experience.

OK, now let's talk about salvation. Traditional Christianity teaches that Jesus Christ died for our sins and is our salvation. In this teaching, we are told that there is no death and salvation is "the undoing of what never was." (W43.2:3) It is the remembrance of the Holy Spirit in our mind that returns us to sanity and peace. We are saved each time we discern an unloving thought and shift away from it to our right mind. So, we don't have to feel guilty that Jesus died to save us. He did not die because he lives forever in the mind of Creation with us. While in the dream body, He remembered his True Identity and stands as a role model and elder brother to help us obtain the same awareness. And we don't have to be crucified to learn this. Accepting the ego as our guide has been punishment enough!

Our lesson says we cannot see apart from God. This flies in the face of our experience. We certainly don't seem to be thinking with God a good deal of the time. Angry, fearful, jealous, depressed thoughts are not God's thoughts. These are perceptions of the ego. That we seem to "see" these things is the reason we need the Holy Spirit to help return us to our right mind.

The Holy Spirit teaches us the power of forgiveness, which is another fundamental concept of our study program. In forgiving the trespasses we see in others, we release the chains of our own unforgiveness. There are many lessons that focus specifically on forgiveness. We will speak of this in great detail as we go along.

Perhaps you've noticed how gently our Teacher instructs us in each lesson. We are given directions, yet it is clear that our Teacher knows we will have difficulty following them perfectly. In the longer practice periods, we are being led step-by-step to take back control over our thoughts—to learn to set our focus and keep it there since we are so easily distracted.

"Try today not to allow any long periods of time to slip by without remembering today's idea." He knows we have long lapses but it's not a sin! *We* are the only ones who suffer as a result of our forgetfulness. We are learning to catch our wayward, unhealthy thoughts and shift instead to thoughts that join us to one another with respect and compassion. We do this each time we can apply the thought for the day to ourself and to everyone we meet.

Reader Reflection/Action

In your quiet times today, practice imagining that you are in partnership with God or the Holy Spirit. As a good partner, you want to be thinking along the same lines. What thoughts of yours will you want to keep, and which do you want to release? Affirm, as often as possible today, that God is your Source.

Lesson 44

God is the light in which I see.

Our lesson today continues the idea of mind training that we began in Lesson 42, when we discussed brainwashing. The Introduction to the Workbook says, "The purpose of the workbook is to train your mind in a systematic way to a different perception of everyone and everything in the world." (WIntro.4) Our Teacher tells us this must be done before we will be able to truly see (i.e., with vision).

The *Course* often uses analogies to give us a picture to aid our understanding. Light and darkness are analogous to the right mind and the ego. We can only see in light: "You cannot see in darkness and you cannot make light. You can make darkness and then think you see in it . . .." (W44.1:2) So, the ego has made its own version of light (the sun) and a body with eyes to see it. In our ego mind, we never question the validity of this kind of seeing.

Notice that we "cannot make light." Light is God's Creation of which we are all a part. That we don't see ourself as that Light is the reason for this training. Elsewhere our Teacher tells us that the only difference between us and God is that He created us. We didn't create Him. God is First Cause and we are the Effect. Cause and effect cannot be separated so, if God created Light, then we are that Light. This is extremely important in terms of understanding our relationship to God and to each other.

The ego would have us believe that we create ourself through the act of procreation. And if bodies were eternal, then we would be true creators. However, bodies perish and are not eternal, Everything of God is eternal. All else is transitory and therefore, illusion.

There are many aspects to the training we are receiving from this curriculum. We are learning a specific vocabulary in order to understand the concepts that are fundamental to achi*eving peace*. We are learning ideas that we have never before entertained. And we are being taught various techniques to rein in our unruly mind.

Over the last 6 weeks, we have been gently led along the path of inner reflection. Initially, we were asked to merely repeat an idea two times a day. Then the number of repetitions increased so that now we are to remember the idea for the day as frequently as possible, every 10 minutes is suggested. Unless you are a realized being, you've probably found it difficult (if not impossible) to remember that often. Your ego will attempt to make you feel guilty and like a failure. Of course! That's what egos are best at doing. You can *and must* choose to relinquish that guilt, then recommit yourself to doing the best you can.

All of these instructions have been guiding us to where we can "observe our passing thoughts without involvement (or guilt) and slip quietly by them." We have been building our spiritual muscles so that we can enter into that deep well of stillness at the core of our being without fear. We are steadily preparing to meet our own True Self!

Reader Reflection/Action ~

Light represents truth, joy, peace, unity. In your quiet time today, ask yourself, "How much Light do i see?" Write down the incident, thing, or person you saw in Light. And, as always, spend the day acknowledging your partnership with God or the Holy Spirit as frequently as possible.

Lesson 45

God is the Mind with which I think.

Today's lesson has us immersed in our relationship to God, which is the only loving relationship there is! The radical nature of our study is evident in what we read today: "Your thoughts are in the Mind of God, as you are. They are in your mind as well, where HE IS [my caps]." (W45.2:6) In a nutshell, we are one with God!! His thoughts are our thoughts and ours are His.

This doesn't seem to make sense—is God thinking about my money problems or my codependent relationships? The *Course* says, no, God's thoughts are eternal and cannot have anything to do with this mundane, physical world. God did not create this world and therefore has no thoughts about it. We, on the other hand, think we have thoughts about a world separate from God, but as we have been learning, the ego thoughts we think, which keep us separate from our Source and from each other, are not real thoughts. (See Lessons 8 and 10.)

One analogy offered is that we have fallen asleep and are having a dream in which there are millions of characters, each separate and different, that we interact with in various levels and degrees. Our interactions, and the ego-based thoughts underlying them, are fraught with intrigue and anxiety. They are the wild imaginings of a misguided mind; a mind that pictures itself as an autonomous individual- unique, alone and vulnerable.

Yet thoughts cannot leave their Source, nor can we be apart from God. Our real thoughts exist in the right part of our mind as they always have. These thoughts that are aligned with God's would have us do what God wills for us. And we, being part of God, only want to do His will. His will for us is perfect happiness, as a later lesson will discuss.

Our Teacher assures us that we will remember God's will for us by following His instructions. The purpose of our practice is to connect once more to that part of the mind which is ever one with its Source. It is here that we will find the happiness and peace we have long sought.

By now we are able to recognize the myriad random thoughts that flood our mind unbidden. We've been practicing relinquishing these meaningless thoughts because we see them and appreciate their lack of value. Making a space, we can now allow the real thoughts of endless comfort and serenity to enter into our consciousness bringing unspeakable joy, even if it lasts a fleeting moment. We will string these miracles together until they are a seamless, gleaming strand leading us Home.

Reader Reflection/Action ~

In your quiet times today, do something a little different. Rather than trying to observe your ego thoughts, imagine you are slipping past them down into a sacred grotto. In this holy place, you can hear your real thoughts . . . the ones you think with God. For a few minutes, listen in awe and gratitude. If you can't get to the grotto today, forgive yourself and continue to monitor your ego thoughts. As you go through the day, observe a thought and ask yourself, "Would God think this thought?"

Lesson 46

God is the Love in which I forgive.

If i had to describe what ACIM is all about in *one* word, it would be *forgiveness*. Forgiveness is the foundation principle of ACIM. As you will see, the Workbook spends quite a bit of time and a number of lessons clarifying what forgiveness is and why it is so important.

Forgiveness is only necessary in a world of duality where it seems possible to condemn or be condemned or judged by another. (And who of us here hasn't found fault with someone?) It is only in duality that there can be anger, fear, or any emotion—all of which are products of projection. We know we have accepted duality because we apparently live in a world of unlimited choices. Nothing is simple. There are people all around us who cause us pain in one form or another.

Forgiveness is the solution to all our problems. It lets reality be present, discharging the false images of the ego back into the nothingness from which they came. "Those who forgive are thus releasing themselves from illusions, while those who withhold forgiveness are binding themselves to them." (W46.1:4) The refusal to forgive keeps us in the ego's chains.

Despite what Genesis says, God could never condemn us because we have never left Him to go off and do bad things. Only the ego tells this story that begins with Adam and Eve and continues to this day. It is a story based on the "reality" of separation that the *Course* says never happened. It only seems as if we left home and made a world that God could not enter to judge and punish us. In this place, it is possible to hurt or be hurt. And, so, there is a need for forgiveness.

Others teach that we should pray to God for forgiveness. The *Course* teaches that God has already forgiven us. However, we do not accept God's forgiveness because we continue to condemn our self for the grievances we seemingly hold against others. Our real problem is not forgiving others but rather, ourself for the imagined "sin" of walking out on God.

Unfortunately, our ego is completely unaware of this. In taking the ego's hand, we have effectively forgotten our complicity in making a world where God cannot be found.

That is why we need the Holy Spirit to show us the way home. God gave us the Holy Spirit as an antidote for our forgetfulness. Each time we ask the Holy Spirit's help in shifting from victim to lover, we move a bit closer to home. Each act of forgiveness paves another step on the "journey without distance." Our apparent departure from Heaven is the birth of all other sins. Forgiveness is our rebirth! This may not make sense now but in time it will!

Reader Reflection/Action ~

In your quiet times today, think of what forgiveness means to you. Write down your definition. Then, close your eyes and picture the face of an "enemy," someone you hold a grudge against or simply dislike. Can you see yourself forgiving this person? And, as usual, go through the day feeling the Presence of God with you. You are holy!

Lesson 47

God is the strength in which I trust.

Our lesson today doesn't say, "God gives me the strength to trust." No, it says God *is* the strength in which i trust. I trust when i return my awareness to my oneness with God. Then it is with God's strength that i trust. The ego cannot trust. It can only make alliances to serve its own interests, but the pact it makes is not based on trust but expedience and risk taking. The ego is always ready to be disappointed, lied to, and/or betrayed. And often it is, because projection makes perception.

So, we have good reason to be anxious and fearful because of the decision we are making to accept the ego's plan for living. Our wrong mind, where the ego has set up shop, is bent on our slow, agonizing demise with a few happy moments sprinkled in to keep us tethered to the hope that continuous pleasure is right around the corner; that we can control the people and events in our life; that we can make everything finally come out right.

The ego lies, as we probably are well aware, at least in others. We are exceptionally well versed in lying to ourself and then denying that we've done so. These self-delusions are particularly painful to acknowledge and a reason why so many find this discipline so difficult. *This teaching* implores us to choose God's Voice instead: "God is your safety in every circumstance. His Voice speaks for Him in all situations . . . telling you exactly what to do to call upon His strength and His protection." (W47.3)

Our Teacher tells us that in order to correct our erroneous thinking, we must first see the frailty in our mind. However, there is a curious dichotomy about the *Course*: we need to develop a fairly confident ego before we can begin to relinquish it to the Holy Spirit. The decision to let the ego go must be made with a clear assertion or it will not truly be accomplished. Put another way, we must be able to say, "I thought i knew what was right but now i see that i was wrong." The ego lacking self-worth would never be able to admit it could be wrong.

Why should we not trust our own (ego) strength? Let's look at the characteristics of our God as described from Lesson 43 up to now: God is Source, God is Light, God is Mind, God is Love, God is limitless Strength. Are any of these characteristics dependent on a body? Do we believe we possess all of these qualities? We may squirm a bit trying to answer this question as we may find it difficult in all truthfulness to assert that we currently possess all these characteristics. Yet we can trust in this . . . where is the Kingdom of Heaven? In our right mind, which *is* one with its Source.

Reader Reflection/Action ~

Here's a silly question: Do you think that God gets tired? You're laughing, right? Only if we endow God with human faults, as the Bible does. Can the eternal ever get tired? Or angry? Or jealous? Obviously, then, God's strength is greater than ours. So why would we want to use our own puny strength when we have the power of God at our service? Ponder this in your quiet times today.

Lesson 48

There is nothing to fear.

Today we are brought right up against our resistance. Your ego is quite probably saying, "This lesson goes too far. How can it say that there is *nothing* to fear?! Any half-witted person knows that there are many things we should fear if we are to stay alive."

Our Teacher is not suggesting that we throw caution to the wind and make no plans, or not buy insurance or not go to the doctor. He is not saying, don't look before you cross the street, or don't make sure your kids brush their teeth, etc., etc. We certainly should do all the things that need doing as we live our days in this world we made.

What the *Course is* saying is to do everything with God's strength and not your own weakness. This entails first acknowledging that you are weak. It is very hard to do this because we have been taught to stand alone, to trust no one completely, and to depend on our own resources to find the answers to our questions (except for Google!).

We know we are relying on our own strength (or lack thereof) when fear enters our mind. This fear can come in many forms such as uncertainty, distress, sadness, euphoria, embarrassment, anger, dissatisfaction, giddiness, annoyance, and so on. Because we are on ego-automatic, the ego always speaks first, so we will experience the fear that is continually arising in our daily routines as a matter of habit.

The initial goal of these lessons is not to expect that our fearful thoughts will disappear, but rather to notice them as quickly as possible and then ask the Holy Spirit for a correction. The faster we realize we don't want to depend on our own limited strength, and to ask for the Holy Spirit's help instead, the sooner we will release our fearful thoughts and attain the peace we seek.

What would give us the confidence to trust the Holy Spirit instead of the ego? A number of things: discontent with the answers our ego gives, the comprehension that the Holy Spirit is not something 'other' but actually the right part of our own mind; a weariness of thinking and doing the same things and expecting a different result (the definition of insanity!) to list a few.

If we're going to be fearless, we must step outside the box our ego made for us, despite the trepidation we feel. Practice makes perfect. As we enlarge spiritual muscles (by doing our lessons) we begin to see the limitations we have put around ourself.

What an eye-opener when we clearly behold for the first time, a thought in our mind that is causing us pain! Then knowing there is One Who can remove the pain by helping us shift our perception is the greatest of gifts, beyond price! When we invite the Holy Spirit into our awareness, there can be no fear because we are utilizing the strength of God.

Reader Reflection/Action

Spend your quiet times today seeking out all the many fears that ceaselessly follow you around. You know what they are. Write them down. Are you willing to give them to the Holy Spirit for correction? As often as you can today, notice a fear, a doubt, a judgment, and say to yourself, "There is nothing to fear because God is with me."

Lesson 49

God's Voice speaks to me all through the day.

All our work until this point is to make today's lesson a reality. We attain the goal of the curriculum, which is the Peace of God, when we are constantly in dialogue with the Holy Spirit, (the Voice for God) in our mind.

By now, we should be aware of our ego resistance to disciplined study. We forget the lesson we so fervently studied this morning! The whole day goes by and then we suddenly remember that we forgot to do the lesson through the day. Sound familiar?

We are attempting to perform very holy work which enrages the ego; to "Go past all the raucous shrieks and sick imaginings that cover your real thoughts and obscure your eternal link with God." (W49.4:3) The ego becomes suspicious as soon as it sees us turning away from its guidance. This is when we must be strong in our determination because the ego will throw at us exactly what it knows will grab our attention and pull us back into its realm of influence.

The greatest teacher in the world cannot and would not force a student to learn hir lessons. It is up to us, as the student, to determine the course of study we wish to pursue and then apply ourself as single-mindedly as possible to its wisdom. Students who try to mix different schools of thought become confused. I remember my Intro to Philosophy course in college. When it was over i kept getting Kant's ideas mixed up with Hume's. Too much information in too little time.

So, the attempt to blend different philosophies will covertly undermine our confidence in the material we've chosen, as if to say, "This *Course* is not enough . . . there needs to be some addition. All the wisdom necessary for transformation can't be in just this one teaching." This can and does lead to deletions that don't fit our criteria (or beliefs) as well. We omit principles of the philosophy that don't mesh with our sensibilities. Or we reinterpret them so that they fit our needs.

The ego adores this! The stealthy aim of the ego is to have you pick one from column A and one from column B thereby diluting both teachings. In effect, you are designing your own philosophy! You can't choose that 1 + 1 = 2 and then decide that 2 × 2 = 5. My teacher Ken said many times, "Stay true to this study or find something else, but don't mix!"

This doesn't mean that we, as *Course* students, can't read other books on spirituality. I've read hundreds. But be sure not to say that the *Course* is just like _____ (some other spirituality). There are many paths through which to hear God's Voice. Each one needs our complete devotion if we are to reach its goal. This is a time for commitment and trust!

Reader Reflection/Action ~

At Lesson 49, our Teacher doesn't really expect us to be listening to God's Voice all day long. But he does want to instill the idea that we can and will develop this relationship. In your quiet times today, try to reach the grotto, that holy place deep below all the noisy, jangling ego thoughts in your mind. It is here that you will hear God's Voice assuring you of His love and devotion. And, again, don't let guilt at lack of success stop you. Guilt is an ego thought and, therefore, not real.

Lesson 50

I am sustained by the Love of God.

"Only the Love of God will protect you in all circumstances," (W50.3) because only the remembrance of God's Love activates our right mind where peace prevails over all illusions. We recall God's Love by first apprehending all the ego thoughts that come to mind so effortlessly and then relinquishing them. As long as they remain uppermost in our attention, we will be unable to see anything else.

The ego assures us that it knows how to protect us. It has three main lines of defense: attack or projection, denial, and avoidance. Our ego tends to favor one technique of defense over the others but all three are used regularly.

- Attack: Ego says the best defense is a good offense so it counsels us to show strength by being aggressive in manner and speech as well as projecting our fear onto another body. This works especially well when we are unsure of ourself. By running roughshod over others, we delay or halt discussion or resolution. Attack can take more subtle forms such as illness or depression. In this case, it says, "Look what you've done to me."

- Denial: When confronted with unpleasant information, we simply pretend we didn't see it or hear it. It doesn't go away but is pushed underground where it festers and eventually explodes in an attack.

- Avoidance: Did you ever turn your back when you saw someone you didn't want to talk to? The ego is a master of back-turning on issues that are fearful. A subtext of avoidance is minimizing. By making light of a situation, we can consider it not worth our time at the moment, but we know it will return to haunt us in the future.

The main purpose of all ego defenses is to keep us rooted in our bodies and out of our mind. It is the body that needs money, pills, and power to feel safe. What the ego never accepts is that all the "stuff" in the world will not assure a peaceful mind. And no defense will work completely because its goal is to save the body, not the mind.

The practice instruction is codified today. We are to:

- Repeat the idea for the day, morning, evening, and frequently through the day.

- Think about what it means.

- Let related thoughts come forward.

- Sink into the holy place.

- Banish idle thoughts and revel in the peace that has always been there.

Faith in the power of God's Love brings us ever nearer to the peace and joy we desire!

First 50 Lessons Epilogue

We've come to the end of the first 50 lessons—the "weed pluckers," as my first teacher Paul used to call them. Their job has been to shake up our indolent mind—to get it to start asking real questions about who we are and what this life is all about, to begin the process of removing the old ideas we have, so that these new ideas can find a home.

Perhaps you were startled to learn that

1. Nothing in this world means anything because it is not real.
2. You are never upset for the reason you think.
3. Nobody can hurt you unless you allow it.
4. You don't perceive your own best interests.
5. God, or the Holy Spirit, is in your mind.
6. Your mind is not the brain.
7. You have invented the world.
8. Your mind is part of God's.
9. You are holy.

Just to mention a few!

If you're still having trouble digesting these radical concepts, i'm not surprised! In fact, i'd be surprised if you weren't. We are at the beginning of the study. There is no rush. You can take all the time you need to finish the lessons. However, if you quit, your ego probably retained you in its grasp. That's not a crime or a sin but it is a shame, especially since you don't have to suffer any longer.

You have received your invitation to the Holy Spirit in your right mind. This is a gift you may have little real appreciation for at this moment, but as you travel along, the magnitude of that gift will grow on you.

My continuous conversations with the Holy Spirit and Jesus have been the lift in my wings as i soar above the leaden ego, freeing its chains from my mind. This is my chosen path. I'm so glad you are traveling with me!

GodisLove

Marcia Grace

Loving power fills my being
When I'm in touch with me
When I'm true to what I'm feeling
I can set my spirit free
Peace and harmony fully flow
Giving strength to my body
Loving power shines within me
And around me—Blessed be!

Review I:
Lessons 51 to 60

~

Review I: Review of Lessons 1 to 50

As in all courses of study, a review period helps the student and the teacher assess how much has been learned. I decided to use this as a separate day and go on to Lesson 51 tomorrow. There will be other days where i will stop to discuss passages that come up between the lessons. These days can be used to work on your mind-training exercise or repeat a favorite lesson. There is no wrong way to do the lessons as long as you do them in succession and study only one per day.

Our lessons have been helping us to understand that we are all students and teachers to each other as we go about our daily activities. Every encounter offers an opportunity for forgiveness of the other and of ourself. The new ideas we are studying are building our spiritual muscles so that we more often use our inner spiritual strength (which comes from joining with the Holy Spirit in our mind) to solve our perceived problems.

We are being trained to look at all life situations in a different way, to see them as extensions of our own thoughts. We are learning that the responsibility for what we see and experience is in our own mind. This is a great gift even though it can seem like a huge responsibility. If we are victims of other people's actions, then we are helpless. Fear is an appropriate reaction.

But if we recognize that we made the problem, then we can unmake it. Fear becomes an impediment to be relinquished. We are learning to take back the power of decision in our mind.

This mind training process we are undergoing is restoring us to our true nature as God's holy creation, not separate from but eternally a part of our Source. We are told there is nothing outside God, therefore there is nothing outside of us. "You will yet learn that peace is part of you, and requires only that you be there to embrace any situation in which you are. And, finally, you will learn that there is no limit to where you are, so that your peace is everywhere, as you are." (W Review1.5)

In truth, this is no big deal. We eat every day, in fact several times, we work, we sleep. Nothing remarkable. Yet, for me, making a daily year-long commitment to do a lesson a day was a daunting idea at first. I didn't know if i could stay the course! But it's 50 lessons later and despite computer glitches, family emergencies, and life in general, i've managed to express my thoughts about one lesson each day. I feel energized, uplifted, focused, and delighted that this has been relatively easy.

This brings to mind a line from the Text: T14.IV.6:2: "When you have learned how to decide with God, all decisions become as easy and as right as breathing. There is no effort, and you will be led as gently as if you were being carried down a quiet path in summer." Well, i don't know about the summer part (right now it's about 46 degrees outside!) but i certainly do feel loved and gently guided.

Now, let's review these first 50 lessons, the "weed pluckers." Their radical ideas are meant to shake us and wake us up to the beauty and joy that exist outside of our leaden ego. We may not instantly agree with or understand each lesson, yet something deep down says, "Keep going. This is good stuff!"

The review will remind us of our initial reaction to each lesson. Now, as we read the lesson again, we can discern how much of these ideas are beginning to settle into our mind and thoughts, giving us hope for the first time that there is another way of looking at the world, one that inspires peace and joy rather than fear and guilt.

Each day we will review 5 lessons. So, for the next 10 days, feel yourself slowing down and savoring what you have received thus far from your study and reflection.

Lesson 51

Review I: Lessons 1–5

Spend some quiet time reading and thinking about these brief explanations and any related thoughts. Then take any or all of them into your day, thinking of them frequently. You are learning to install these different ideas into your database of beliefs!

Lesson 1. Nothing I see means anything.

"What I think I see now is taking the place of vision." (W51.1:4)

We are on ego-automatic. We see everything through its filter and everything the ego looks upon comes from the belief in separation and is therefore not true. Accepting this is so, we can ask for its correction so true vision can return to our mind.

Lesson 2. I have given what I see all the meaning it has for me.

"I have judged everything I look upon, and it is this and only this I see. This is not vision." (W51.2)

If i want true vision i must be determined to recognize that my judgments are hurting me. I must be willing to leave a space for the truth to be felt, seen and lived instead.

Lesson 3. I do not understand anything I see.

"What I see is a projection of my own errors of thought." (W51.3:3)

This is all we need to know to want to change our mind. The hard part is admitting we are wrong. Egos don't like to do this! The fear is that it will be so ashamed of its stupid actions that it will want to die. And it will, with the help of the Holy Spirit.

Lesson 4. These thoughts do not mean anything.

"The thoughts of which I am aware do not mean anything because I am trying to think without God." (W51.4:2)

Our real thoughts lie hidden under the judgmental thoughts of the ego. All our efforts should be directed at noticing our ego thoughts for what they are and then wanting to change our mind.

Lesson 5. I'm never upset for the reason I think.

"I make all things my enemies, so that my anger is justified and my attacks are warranted." (W51.5:4)

We are tired and upset because we are working so hard to make our false ideas true. This is an exhausting and frustrating activity that brings us nothing but pain. We are beginning to realize we do not have to suffer. We can let go of damaging thoughts and be at peace

Lesson 52

Review I: Lessons 6–10

Read, reflect, and think often of one or more of these lessons during the day.

Lesson 6. I am upset because I see what is not there.

"When I am upset, it is always because I have replaced reality with illusions I made up." (W52.1:5)

I think of becoming upset as something that happens *to* me, against my will and not in my control. These lessons are teaching just the opposite—i am choosing to be upset because i fear God's peace, having taken the ego's hand as my guide.

Lesson 7. I see only the past.

"When I have forgiven myself and remembered who I am, I will bless everyone and everything I see." (W52.2:5)

I am waking up! I no longer want to condemn anyone because

i realize it keeps me separate from my siblings who share my perfect holiness.

Lesson 8. My mind is preoccupied with past thoughts.

"Let me remember that I look on the past to prevent the present from dawning on my mind." (W52.3:4)

As i allow my right mind to help me release the past, i see there truly is no value in holding onto it. Holding on to the past is my ego's way of making time a reality, separating me from the truth of Who i am and Who all my siblings are as eternal beings.

Lesson 9. I see nothing as it is now.

"What I have chosen to see has cost me vision. Now I would choose again that I may see." (W52.4:5-6)

How wonderful it is to start to see that all the judgmental thoughts i think that i'm thinking, have no effect and are nothing at all. I am exchanging the darkness of my guilt for the light of vision!

Lesson 10. My thoughts do not mean anything.

"I have no private thoughts. Yet it is only private thoughts of which I am aware." (W52.5)

The belief that my little, private thoughts are real, and as a result are important, is the ego's clever scheme to convince me that bodies and minds are multitudinous in this world. These false thoughts deny the grandeur that is mine as God's holy creation. Why would i want to keep them?

Lesson 53

Review I: Lessons 11–15

Today's five review lessons focus on the insanity of the ego. I've known people to get upset with passages that say things like, "Anyone who elects a totally insane guide must be totally insane himself." (T9.IV.8) The ego doesn't enjoy being called insane because it perceives it as an attack. The Course contains many psychological terms and concepts because it was filtered through the minds of its channels, Helen and Bill, who were clinical psychologists at Columbia Presbyterian Hospital in NYC in the 1960s. In fact, when Helen heard the Voice tell her to "take dictation" she thought she was going crazy. Bill counseled her, "Let's see what it says . . ."

The result was A Course in Miracles.

Lesson 11. My meaningless thoughts are showing me a meaningless world.

"Since the thoughts of which I am aware do not mean anything, the world that pictures them can have no meaning." (W53.1:2)

Meaninglessness and insanity are synonyms in this teaching. My insane ego thoughts manifest a correspondingly insane world of pain and fear. But insane thoughts are not real and since i have real thoughts in my mind as well, i can choose them instead, returning to sanity.

Lesson 12. I am upset because I see a meaningless world.

"I am grateful that the world is not real, and that I need not see it at all unless I choose to value it." (W53.2:6)

At this stage of the study, i simply need to be aware of my guilty, hateful, anxious thoughts and the pain they are causing me. When i affirm that the chaos of this perceived world is no longer what i want, then i can make a new choice for thoughts of joining and peace.

Lesson 13. A meaningless world engenders fear.

"The totally insane engenders fear because it is completely undependable, and offers no grounds for trust." (W53.3:2)

The very nature of insanity is instability. The ego world harbors no safe haven to rest without fear. That is why i want to recognize its bare unreality and then let it go back to nothingness, replaced by the reality of peace.

Lesson 14. God did not create a meaningless world.

"Why should I continue to suffer from the effects of my own insane thoughts when the perfection of creation is my home?" (W53.4:5)

This is the foundational question i am being led to ask over and over until i realize that the ego holds nothing that i want or need. My Creator created me to share the joy of unity. This world i see is the epitome of division and dis-ease. Therefore, it has no place in my mind.

Lesson 15. My thoughts are images that I have made.

"The fact that I see a world in which there is suffering and loss and death, shows me that I am seeing only the representation of my insane thoughts, and am not allowing my real thoughts to cast their beneficent light on what I see." (W53.5:4)

My will is one with God's, and so, the time will come when i give up this insane desire for autonomy and return to my true state of being. I am free to choose chaos or peace but i am not free to choose my reality as God's Holy Creation.

Lesson 54

Review I: Lessons 16–20

Today's main idea is central to the teaching that all thoughts are shared. People often ask me if i believe in mind readers (or psychics). Yes! We are all mind readers at times. Who hasn't had the experience of knowing what someone else was going to say or do? Most of us don't cultivate the ability because it is threatening to the ego which strives to keep us aloof and defensive, "safe" in our autonomy and "private thoughts."

Lesson 16. I have no neutral thoughts.

"Neutral thoughts are impossible because all thoughts have power." (W54.1:2)

All thinking has an effect. As i allow my mind to wander in fearful thinking (what ifs, i should'ves), i attract like-minded individuals who relish disaster. (Birds of a feather flock together!) By catching those thoughts and asking for their transformation, i draw more serene, nonviolent relationships to me.

Lesson 17. I see no neutral things.

"Let me look on the world I see as a representation of my own state of mind." (W54.2:4)

As difficult as it is to imagine that i can see the people and situations in my life differently, i am willing to conceive of the possibility. I MUST envision it in order for there to be a change. It is only *my* mind that can bring a new perception of the world i see. Because i am on ego-automatic, until i ask for change i will participate in loneliness, fatigue, melancholy, and worthlessness, among other delights of the ego.

Lesson 18. I am not alone in experiencing the effects of my seeing.

"As my thoughts of separation call to the separation thoughts of others, so my real thoughts awaken the real thoughts in them. And the world my real thoughts show me will dawn on their sight as well as mine." (W54.3:6-7)

Since there is no separation, what i believe is what i will project onto others. It doesn't seem to be so because i see different aspects of my chaotic thinking in different people. Yet, when i decide with my right mind, i will see and experience loving interactions with everyone around me.

Lesson 19. I am not alone in experiencing the effects of my thoughts.

"I am alone in nothing. Everything I think or say or do teaches all the universe." (W54.4:2-3)

May i always be asking the Holy Spirit to guide me in the right and proper channels. Since i am connected to everyone else, i will experience the effects of my thoughts on others. If i radiate anger, that is what i will receive. If i radiate love and acceptance, that is what i will receive.

Lesson 20. I am determined to see.

"I would behold the proof that what has been done through me has enabled love to replace fear, laughter to replace tears, and abundance to replace loss." (W54.5:4)

Because i want the peace of God, i must want it also for my sibling travelers on the journey home. It is they who show me what i am thinking. My thoughts become the actions of my companions on the path. My gratitude for what they teach me showers me with miracles!

Lesson 55

Review 1: Lessons 21-25

Our lessons today center on our faulty perception that stems from having forgotten Who we are in truth. Under these circumstances, how can we possibly have our own best interests in mind?

Lesson 21. I am determined to see things differently.

"I am determined to see the witnesses to the truth in me, rather than those which show me an illusion of myself." (W55.1:7)

One radical teaching of the Course is that God did not create the world or anything in it. He did not create me as a separate body on my own in the universe. If i see myself in this way, then i do not understand my Creator or myself. God could not create division, being the God of Love.

Lesson 22. What I see is a form of vengeance.

"The world I see is hardly the representation of loving thoughts. It is a picture of attack...It is my own attack thoughts that give rise to this picture. (W55.2:2)

The ego in me works 24/7 to keep strife alive in my thoughts. Yet there is a part of my mind untouched by its alienating influences, the part that has never separated from God, to which i can return the instant i am willing to give up the meager offerings of the ego.

Lesson 23. I can escape from this world by giving up attack thoughts.

"As forgiveness allows love to return to my awareness, I will see a world of peace and safety and joy." (W55.3:4)

Forgiveness is the unfailing tool i have been given by my Teacher to resolve all disharmony in my mind. W.Pt ll.1.4:1-3 says, "Forgiveness . . . is still, and quietly does nothing . . . . It merely looks, and waits, and judges not." All of these characteristics—stillness, nonreaction, patience, nonjudgment—are all antithetical to the ego. When i practice these i am retraining my mind in a way that will transform my relationships, bringing me to a state of unassailable peace.

Lesson 24. I do not perceive my own best interests.

"I am willing to follow the Guide God has given me to find out what my own best interests are, recognizing that I cannot perceive them by myself." (W55.4:4)

To get a job done right, i need the proper tools and, just as importantly, an expert to show me what to do. My Teacher gives me forgiveness as the tool, and the Holy Spirit as the Guide who will lead me in straight paths. My decision to ask the Holy Spirit's help is the necessary shift that brings me to my right mind. It is here that i remember who i AM.

Lesson 25. I do not know what anything is for.

"The purpose I have given the world has led to a frightening picture of it." (W55.5:6)

I have been overtly as well as subtly taught by my family and teachers that the world is dangerous and i must be prepared to defend myself at all times. This reactive thinking has substituted for my real thoughts which see only loving relationships, or ones that require healing and nothing else. When i look on the things of the world with new eyes, i do not feel alone for i know my Helper is with me. Together we choose peace.

Lesson 56

Review I: Lessons 26–30

Our lessons today concentrate on how our faulty sense of self leads to suffering. One of the major differences i see in this path from other spiritual philosophies is its focus on our misperceptions, flawed judgments, and misbegotten assumptions. Whereas many other disciplines fixate on the positive aspects of life, our study asks us to summon the honesty and courage to reveal all our hidden hates and buried fears. They must be brought to the light and transformed so that we may return to a state of permanent peace.

Lesson 26. My attack thoughts are attacking my invulnerability.

"All my hopes and wishes and plans appear to be at the mercy of a world I cannot control." (W56.1:4)

I seem to be under continual attack from sources outside my influence. The huge open secret here is that it is my own attack thoughts that are causing me distress in many forms. I forget who i *am* every time i take umbrage at something someone says, every time i get upset because something isn't going my way, every time i look out and see a competitor trying to beat me. I make up these images to hide the light in me. But now i'm waking up (or at least stirring from sleep) and getting ready to exchange attack for peace.

Lesson 27. Above all else I want to see.

"Recognizing that what I see reflects what I think I am, I realize that vision is my greatest need." (W56.2:2)

When the truth dawns clearly that only my own beliefs are keeping me in hell, then i begin the typically slow progression (called the Atonement process) of bringing to my attention all the blocks to peace that i invent. Seeing these clearly, i can then ask the Holy Spirit to help correct my misperceptions.

Lesson 28. Above all else I want to see things differently.

"While i see the world as i see it now, truth cannot enter my awareness." (W56.3:3)

I remember many years ago, when my life seemed to be in shambles. I was stricken with unbearable pain and i cried to God, "i want to see things differently." Over and over i repeated the words like a mantra, not really knowing what i was saying but with a rudimentary awareness that something had to change. It took me quite a while to realize that i only have to *want* to change my mind: that is enough. I don't have to know how it will happen. The clear desire opens the door to the miracle that heals my mind.

Lesson 29. God is in everything I see.

"Beyond all my insane wishes is my will, united with the will of my Father." (W56.4:4)

I have a choice as to how i see all people and events in my life. This is so easy to say yet so hard to put into practice. Most of the time, because i'm on ego-automatic, i don't even consider that there is another way to view my situation. My beliefs are so entrenched that it often takes a major disturbance (tragedy, trauma) to lead me to ask for help to lift me out of the hole i have dug myself into. This *must* happen eventually, since my will is always one with God's. I cannot remain forever in hell.

Lesson 30. God is in everything I see because God is in my mind.

"I have not lost the knowledge of Who I am because I have forgotten it. It has been kept for me in the Mind of God, Who has not left His Thoughts." (W56.5:3)

No matter how terrible my life may seem and how much i suffer, i can ask for a miracle and be renewed. Because God didn't create this veil of tears, there is every reason to relinquish my attachment to it. All i need is the true desire for God's eternal peace, not the ego's, which comes and goes according to the whim of the dream. Waking up is coming home to Reality.

Lesson 57

Review I: Lessons 31–35

It is hardly a stretch to see this world as a prison where we are caged by our defective thought system. The restriction of our spirit leads to power struggles, fury fights, and nonstop defensive maneuvers. Our lessons aim to release the bonds of ego thinking and return us to the awareness of the power of our mind to CHOOSE the path of peace.

Lesson 31. I am not the victim of the world I see.

"Nothing holds me in this world. Only my wish to stay keeps me a prisoner. (W57.1:7)

My first teacher Paul (from 1978–1985) always said, "This course is simple but it's not easy." What could be simpler than changing my mind (but more difficult)? My ego has such an investment in being right that anything that might even slightly seem counter to its preconceived notions, is immediately disarmed, denied, or attacked. This is a main reason why change is so resistible!

Lesson 32. I have invented the world I see.

"I have deluded myself into believing it is possible to imprison the Son of God." (W57.2:4)

My ego claims it wants to learn, grow, and expand my consciousness, yet it must always be on the look-out for possible annihilation. It knows it has an enemy who is endeavoring to win back my mind. So, it must keep a tight rein on my thoughts or else i will break the chains of guilt and fear and return to my right mind, leading to the ego's dissolution.

Lesson 33. There is another way of looking at the world.

"I would look upon the world as it is, and see it as a place where the Son of God finds his freedom." (W57.3:6)

Every time i stop, for even just a second, and question a thought in my mind from a logical, detached point of view, i am shifting my thinking to my right mind. This is the space where miracles are born. The only extra, added ingredient necessary for the realization of the miracle is my collaboration with the Holy Spirit in my mind.

Lesson 34. I could see peace instead of this.

"When I see the world as a place of freedom, I realize that it reflects the laws of God instead of the rules I made for it to obey." (W57.4:2)

The Holy Spirit's presence in my mind is crucial to my receiving a miracle (a change of perception). If i try to do it myself, i am right back in the ego's penitentiary of limited understanding. Because i'm on ego-automatic, i will want the miracle for the wrong reason. Instead, i can choose to see this world as a classroom where i've come to learn the Holy Spirit's curriculum.

Lesson 35. My mind is part of God's. I am very holy.

"I begin to understand the holiness of all living things, including myself, and their oneness with me." (W57.5:5)

With the Holy Spirit as my partner, i am truly in a state of grace and communion with my Source. In my right mind is a new world, the real world, the world transformed. Here suddenly all is forgiven, and all beings are worthy of my compassion. Complete serenity is my vibration! How beautiful, powerful, and freeing is this state!

Lesson 58

Review I: Lessons 36–40

How many of us can say we were brought up to believe we were holy beings? Did our parents remind us of our holiness every day? Did we have lessons in school on how to best utilize our holiness? Although our parents probably loved us and our teachers were well trained, THEY didn't assume their holiness so, how could they promote ours? Now we have a new Teacher to guide us back to our true Identity as God's holy Son.

Lesson 36. My holiness envelopes everything I see.

"From my holiness does the perception of the real world come." (W58.1:2)

The goal of this study is *not* to get to heaven. It isn't? No, because i am already in heaven even though i don't know it. So, the real purpose of my lessons is to shift my perception from the ego, which believes i am a sinner, to my right mind where the awareness of my holiness has always been. Choosing to make this shift brings me to the real world. Heaven is just a step or two away! Heaven is peace of mind.

Lesson 37. My holiness blesses the world.

"There is nothing apart from this joy, because there is nothing that does not share my holiness." (W58.2:4)

The real world is the world i currently see, but transformed. In the real world i am aware that there are others around me but i feel no sense of separation. We are undivided parts of a greater whole which is eternally holy.

Lesson 38. There is nothing my holiness cannot do.

"In the presence of my holiness, which I share with God Himself, all idols vanish." (W58.3:6)

My holiness is the fertile ground where miracles blossom. Holiness shifts my thoughts from self-interest to compassion and service. Where before i saw an angry person, now i see a fearful one; one in need of understanding and love. My holiness sees the vulnerability in others and rushes to comfort and support.

Lesson 39. My holiness is my salvation.

"Since my holiness saves me from all guilt, recognizing my holiness is recognizing my salvation." (W58.4:2)

Salvation is an ancient concept whose form varies relative to the discipline from which it stems. As i study and reflect, i'm learning that my salvation comes from performing miracles!

No one can do this for me, but neither can i do it alone. First i *must want to see a miracle* (a change of perception) and then i must *remember to invite the Holy Spirit in.* Together we dispel the ego's layers of fear, guilt, and sin that seem to hide my True Self from me.

Lesson 40. I am blessed as a Son of God.

"I cannot suffer any loss or deprivation or pain because of Who I am." (W58.5:5)

In traditional Christianity, Jesus is the only Son of God and He suffered and died for our sins. In this teaching, we *all* are God's Son in whom He is well pleased! We are created in joy and peace by our loving Creator so that pain and suffering are impossible. The miracle is the acknowledgment of my true identity as God's blessed Son.

Lesson 59

Review I: Lessons 41–45

All our senses were made to conceal our oneness with God. Our holiness remains hidden in a world of duality made up of our projected thought and acted out in our 5-sensory world. We made a world apart from God because we believed the ego's story that God is angry with us and would punish us if we came home.

These lessons are the antidote to this sick and fearful tale.

Lesson 41. God goes with me wherever I go.

"How can I be disturbed by anything when He rests in me in absolute peace?" (W59.1:4)

Imagine what it would be like to feel the Presence of God with me everywhere i am. The miracle is that perhaps brief, but nonetheless exquisite experience of complete connection with another. And each miracle brings me closer to the time when peace and joy are always with me because I am in God's Presence.

Lesson 42. God is my strength. Vision is His gift.

Let me be willing to exchange my pitiful illusion of seeing for the vision that is given by God." (W59.2:3)

Once i believe i've become an autonomous individual, i accept the ego as my partner and follow unflinchingly all its strictures. It tells me to trust no one. It tells me God is Someone to fear. So only by choosing a different Guide than the ego can i recall the gift of God's vision.

Lesson 43. God is my Source. I cannot see apart from Him.

"It is these [illusions] I choose when I try to see through the body's eyes." (W59.3:6)

My Teacher knows that i have forsaken my true inheritance, manifesting a cruel world based on the ego's plan. He also knows that i am frozen by fear of retaliation and dreaming of war and vengeance. His plan, should i elect to follow Him, will eradicate all fear, leaving a clean slate where vision takes the place of perception.

Lesson 44. God is the Light in which I see.

"Let me welcome vision and the happy world it will show me." (W59.4:7)

The world of my ego is filled with darkness. The real world of the Holy Spirit is bathed in light. In the dark i see defensively.

In the light of truth, vision shows a healed world, one where enemies become soulmates and we walk together in peace.

Lesson 45. God is the Mind with which I think.

"I have no thoughts I do not share with God." (W59.5:2)

The thoughts i think that are private thoughts are simply the illusionary thoughts of the ego. It is the healed world i long to see. But only when i confront my fear of God directly, and see the empty space where i thought His Judgment lurks, will i be convinced that i was wrong. I cannot think apart from my Creator nor can He think apart from me. Our Mind is one in unified creativity.

Lesson 60

Review I: Lessons 46–50

The power of forgiveness, and its necessity for healing the mind, threads its way through our discourse today. We need and want forgiveness for ourself and those we see outside ourself in order to remember the love we share with our Creator.

Lesson 46. God is the Love in which I forgive.

"God does not forgive because He never condemned." (W60.1:2)

When i first read these words i was overcome by their significance and authenticity. "Of course!" i said to myself, "God has never condemned anyone! How could a loving Creator threaten His Creations?" The stories of God's wrath and vengeance are inventions of the ego to keep us in its clutches. Only the ego condemns and projects its judgment onto God. The story the ego has told me is becoming unglued! Perhaps i really don't have to be afraid of God after all!

Lesson 47. God is the strength in which I trust.

"It is not my own strength though which I forgive. It is with the strength of God in me, which I am remembering as I forgive." (W60.2:2)

If God is not an enemy, as my ego has tried to convince me, then i am free to explore my relationship with my Source on a whole new level. On this new ground of being, we are not master and possession but rather the sun and its rays. I am the same "stuff" as my Creator and cannot be separated. In this way i forgive God for what He never did (kick me out of the house) and i forgive myself for believing i could leave. So, His strength can only be mine. Who else is there to trust?

Lesson 48. There is nothing to fear.

"Everyone and everything I see will lean toward me to bless me." (W60.3:4)

What is there to fear when i no longer believe i've been condemned by God? No longer will i need to find another to project my fear upon. Here's a true story: I was visiting a friend one morning. She was giving her little son breakfast and he didn't want to finish eating. His mother admonished him so he went over and kicked the cat! The ego is always looking for someone to victimize. Forgiveness puts an end to projection because my forgiveness sees that there is no harm done and no need to find a victim. In my forgiveness, i see only kindred spirits who share my journey.

Lesson 49. God's Voice speaks to me all through the day.

"There is not a moment in which His Voice fails to direct my thoughts, guide my actions and lead my feet." (W60.4:3)

This is not something i brag about to all my friends—they might put me away if they think i'm hearing voices! Seriously, i must be careful not to take everything that is written literally as some have done with the Bible. Much of the *Course* is written poetically and metaphorically therefore, it is extremely important not to extract a sentence from the material and say, *This* is what the *Course* says. The passage i quote and then interpret must fit into the general scheme set forth in all three volumes of the material. They all hang together. Guidance comes in myriad forms and the more i ask and listen, the better i become at discerning God's Voice from the ego's. Yes, the day will come when I hear only God's Voice and all my illusions will disappear!

Lesson 50. I am sustained by the Love of God.

"As I forgive, His Love reminds me that His Son is sinless." (W60.5:4)

There are so many ways to "hear" the Holy Spirit; the form is not important. It is the clarity and certainty of the guidance that matters. One criteria for true guidance is that it is not for me alone but is helpful to others as well. The guidance i receive from the Holy Spirit or God's Voice is the manifestation of forgiveness. His suggestions are always loving and will show me that my life companions are as sinless as i am.

How Did We Get Here? A Creation Story

~

Students of ACIM can read the book for years and still not understand what it is saying if they haven't heard and comprehended the *Course*'s allegory of creation.

Like the Bible, the *Course* has its own explanation for the appearance of humanity in the world. The story comes in bits and pieces throughout the material, therefore it can easily be glossed over and not recognized for its importance to a true understanding of the principles.

Genesis tells the story of how God creates a man and woman from the dust of the earth and places them in His garden. He tells them they can have everything *except* the fruit of the tree of knowledge. Temptation is born and humanity is set up to endure suffering, fear, and death because of Adam and Eve's sin against God. They eat of the forbidden fruit. And God, in His righteous wrath, expels them with a curse upon His cruel lips. Not a very merry story.

The *Course*'s story, rather than resting on sin, guilt, and fear, has forgiveness and redemption as the major themes. It is a cautionary tale about the vicissitudes of differences, and begins at the end which is now, and proceeds toward the past which never happened!

Once upon a time, minds are joined. Before the *apparent* separation, the Sonship (*all* of us) is one with its Source. In this oneness, all thought is undivided, arising in One Mind. When the separation from God seems to occur, mind becomes split. Now, the mind of God and the mind of the Son are no longer united. The Son has had a thought that there could be something beyond God in Heaven. This thought mesmerizes the Son, "Wow, what would a place outside of God look like?" S/he wonders. And having infinite creativity, the Son begins to imagine a whole new world where God could not be found.

Then the fun seriously begins. (Yes, one of the first splits is the separation of fun and serious!) Once our creative juices get going, the splitting goes into warp speed. From God and the Son come many daughters and sons.

"Wait a minute!" the Son says to Hirself. "God could show up at any moment and bust up all my fantastic imaginings." (Ah, by this point the Son has chosen to forget s/he is one with the Source.) S/he now perceives hirself as many ego individuals and becomes seriously afraid. With God's arrival, His wrath won't be far behind. "We need a better plan," says the Son. "I'll split myself up into multitudinous pieces. That way, God will never be able to find all of me at once!" And the *ego*, or the separated mind, takes precedence in the mind of the Son. Genius!

Necessity being the mother of invention, the Son dreams up the perfect solution: "I'll leave Heaven!" And, voila! s/he manifests a whole space–time continuum, based on the separation of spirit and matter. "The perfect place to hide!" The Son knows this is true because God is spirit and eternal, having no form in time.

Bolstered by hir own cleverness, the Son gets even more creative. A whole environment emerges from hir thoughts: earth, sky, water, air. Plants and animals in almost endless assortments come forth. The Son's greatest coup, the one thing that "proves" hir independence from a now distant and angry God, is hir ability to create hirself! and . . . *bodies* are born! Bodies make bodies without any help from God. Now the Son of God seems to have a body and live in a world of innumerable experiences. This is the coup de grace to God's authority.

And the ego is well pleased. It has manifested its own fabulous kingdom that it rules with an iron hand. No true thought of Love can enter here. The love of this world is contingent upon "special relationships"—alliances with others who strike a bargain with each other to be faithful. Unfortunately, faithfulness is not a trait the ego has in abundance.

All along, this apparent destruction of heavenly unity remains merely a thought! And a misguided one at that! And because it is not a thought of unity, it is not a real thought. Therefore, it can easily be released. The Son in hir dream, imagines s/he has left God's kingdom in favor of hir own. But, in truth, since it is impossible to separate a real thought from the Thinker (God), the supposed separation has *not* occurred.

But tell this to a deranged ego who believes in hir fantasies! (That's us as long as we believe we are egos in this world.) Meanwhile, since Creation is One, there is an instantaneous correction of the Son's errant thought. God, aware of the Son's confusion, had already supplied the answer in a form the Son can utilize: the Holy Spirit, as the solution bringer. The Holy Spirit is nearer than hands or feet; S/he resides in the right part of the Son's mind, ready to be acknowledged.

Unfortunately, the Son turns hir back on It and chooses the ego instead. Yet the Holy Spirit remains with us, faithfully waiting for us to realize the horror of our mistake and ask for correction. Our Creator could never leave us comfortless!
As we learn later on, there is no time, no past or future, only *now*. At this moment, we are still entranced by the idea of a

world where we become the creator because we've banished God. (This is the real story behind Genesis where we project our banishing onto God so that now it is God who has abandoned us.)

So, what is the answer to the dilemma of an ego that believes it has successfully separated itself from the joy of eternal goodness in the name of autonomy?

Let's pick up where we left off with the Son enjoying all the intricacies of bodily life, coming and going, doing and undoing, laughing and crying, living and dying.

After a while, the Son begins to notice how much suffering there is in this world s/he made. The only answer seems to be to bury our misery in false pleasures. But they eventually lose their shine. This is when the Son, hitting the bottom of the barrel, cries out to God, "Help!" Ahh, the one honest statement the Son has made since s/he took on the ego façade. A door has opened, and the light is beginning to trickle in. Waiting patiently in the right part of the Son's mind is the Holy Spirit, ready to give the guidance that will bring the Son back home to the place s/he never left!

Each time we, the Son, feel our pain and ask for help from our inner guidance which is the Holy Spirit, we receive relief in some form of forgiveness. In this particular curriculum, forgiveness is the closest expression of love of which we are currently capable.

Therefore, in a nutshell, God and Creation (Us) are One. Creation has a crazy idea of separation that S/he takes seriously. Feeling guilt at this outrageous thought, the Son invents a hiding place, (the world of physicality, duality, and sin) fearing God's anger. God, Whom the Son has never really left, provides Hir ever-present Love in the Son's distorted thinking with the guidance of the Holy Spirit.

As we, the Son, learn to listen to that guidance, we heal our split mind by forgiving the wrongs we perceive have been done to us. We (the Son) have the ability to wake up from our dream of separation at any time we choose. The only requirement is that we must be willing to admit that we've been wrong. We have *not* left Home; we are *not* separate from our Source, and God is *not* a cruel avenger but rather, our loving Creator Who will never leave us disconsolate!

If you are still with me after today's fairytale, then you must suspect that we have come from some other place and want to know where it is. We'll find it together.

GodisLove

End of the "Weed Pluckers" and on to New Endeavors!

~

When you began this practice, you had many doubts about this course. *Will it help me feel better about myself and my life? Will my anger, jealousy, and fears diminish? Can i truly forgive the people who have hurt me?* This is a perfectly normal reaction for a new student.

Since you've come this far, you realize that all these things are possible even if you haven't completely accomplished them yet. You've had glimpses of ineffable joy and peace each time you've let a miracle replace an ego conviction. Yet, that wonderful feeling quickly dissipates, replaced by another ego thought. The ideas you've invested a lifetime in believing may not depart as quickly as you might hope. This is because your spiritual muscles are not yet strong enough to resist the ego's onslaught. However, deep within, you know that peace is your true inheritance from a loving Creator Who longs for your return to your right mind where all is one.

Now it is time to redouble your commitment to completing the lessons. Your ego will try with all its might to deter you from your chosen path. "You've done enough." It will assure you. "Why don't you try past life regression? . . . or dousing? . . . or sky diving?" It will suggest anything to get you off track and back in its total control. Fight the urge! The ego is not your friend.

The best is yet to come! Each day, as you throw aside another ego belief, your steps become lighter and your goal becomes clearer. The droning voice of the ego becomes fainter. And when you hear it, it becomes a signal, reminding you of what you really want.

I have told you in many ways how much God loves you and has given you all that you need to transform every thought you have of lack and limitation. Don't stop until you can say, without the slightest hesitation, "I am a holy being, clothed in light and filled with joy!"

If you have been doing one lesson a day as i recommended, then you have spent the last 60 days steeped in revelations to shake up your belief system. You should congratulate yourself! These first ideas are antithetical to all your ego stands for, and represent a real threat to it.

What are you feeling? Take some time today to write down what you have learned, what you don't agree with, and what you don't quite understand. If you can be completely honest, you will move along more quickly toward your goal of peace! Resist the urge to sweep your doubts under the carpet of awareness. Much better to drag them into the light of day so you can see them clearly and offer them to your Higher Self, the Holy Spirit in your right mind, for clarification.

Book 2 of *Calm, Creative, Joyful* will introduce you to the second phase of your study of the lessons of *A Course in Miracles*. Your practice will be smoother, more focused, and predetermined. It will have a different rhythm—steadier and eagerly anticipated.

In Book 2, we continue with a new set of lessons and exercises to broaden your learning and support you in the process. Remember, there's no rush. Just because you read a lesson

doesn't mean you grasped its essence. Let yourself savor each day as a precious jewel you are adding to your crown of holiness. Let it sink deep within you. Allow it to give you comfort. Feel the richness of each idea and let it play into your daily thoughts and activities. This study is eminently practical—its goal is for you to be calm, creative, and joyful in your everyday experiences.

If you have enjoyed this journey through the first 50 lessons, order Book 2 to continue on your passage to peace. Your spiritual muscles will carry you along, but they need frequent exercise and the nourishment of your continued willingness to question your beliefs. I applaud your commitment to be the most fulfilled, loving, and blissful being you can be!

Peace and Blessings Always!

Marcia Grace

About the Author

Marcia Grace is an author, speaker, teacher, practical mystic, interfaith minister, grandmother and workshop leader who has been guiding students through *A Course in Miracles* since 1980. She holds weekly classes on Long Island teaching the principles of *A Course in Miracles* and will soon begin a class online where students from anywhere can share their experiences as they learn the concepts of the Course.

She wrote this book to share the valuable lessons she has learned over the years about all the ways our ego tries to keep us in its sharp-clawed grasp, rooted in guilt, and how we can break free to find the calm, creativity and joy within.

Go to www.MarciaGrace.com/guided-meditation-signup/ to hear a free guided meditation given by Marcia Grace.

The Foundation for Inner Peace

To learn more about *A Course in Miracles,* I recommend you visit the website of the authorized publisher and copyright holder of the Course, the Foundation for Inner Peace: www.acim.org. While there are many excellent organizations supporting study of *A Course in Miracles*, this is the original one with the greatest variety and depth of Course-related materials, including biographies and photos of the scribes, DVDs, free access to daily Lessons, audio recordings, information about the many languages into which the Course has been translated, and electronic versions of the Course, including mobile device apps.

The Foundation for Inner Peace is a non-profit organization dedicated to uplifting humanity through *A Course in Miracles*. The organization depends on donations and is currently immersed in translating the Course into many languages (26 to date). The Foundation also donates thousands of copies of the Course. If you would like to support more people to benefit from *A Course in Miracles,* donating to the Foundation for Inner Peace or one of the many other fine Course-related organizations would be a worthy endeavor. A portion of the proceeds from this book will be donated to the Foundation for Inner Peace and other organizations proliferating the message of *A Course in Miracles.*

Made in the USA
San Bernardino, CA
14 August 2018